AUTHORS NOTE

I am a Photojournalist and founder of Funeography® (the funeral photography company). I have been documenting and writing about the world of funerals for over a decade and now I write books on various subjects that interest me. This is the second of what I call PhotoLifebooks.

This book was produced during the Corona virus Pandemic in 2020, the usual interviews conducted face to face have not been allowed. This means that the method of collecting and using personal effects for the book have been very different and challenging. I am grateful that so many victims and relatives of the Hallsville School bombing shared their stories and allowed me to assist in bringing the events back into the limelight with the hope that the many questions asked then and still now will be answered and families may get some closure and an annual public remembrance of the events that occurred.

HALLSVILLE SCHOOL UNCOVERED

LADY PRISCILLA ETIENNE

Published in the United Kingdom,
an imprint of Blurb publishing.
Published in Great Britain by Blurb 2020

Copyright © Lady Priscilla Etienne, 2020

For the military unit, who helped support me
and carried me forward to my own
personal glory.
Formerly The 4th Battalion Royal Green Jackets
West Ham, Portway, London

In Remembrance of Benny Stafford, thanks for all the laughs.

In Remembrance of Pat and Emily Murphy; great-grandparents of my best friend, Sascha.

Acknowledgements

I would like to thank Jenny Stafford for creating the facebook group which inspired this book and the members of the group for sharing their very difficult and heartbreaking stories. A special thank you to Marigold who spoke to me in depth about her life changing experiences and the Feathersone sisters for re-counting their mothers story so beautifuuly.

Photographs

Charles John Canning. P13 Engraved by D.J.Pound, Mayall, Robert Montgomery Martin (1858). .The Indian Empire. Volume 2. London: The London Printing and Publishing Company.

Memorial Headstone for Hallsville School Deceased. P17. South Hallsville School Uncovered. Facebook.com/groups/622945134489555.

World War Bomb, P25 Combined Military Services Museum, Maldon Essex. ©Lady Priscilla Etienne (2020).

A.R.P.Warden Helmet. P31 Combined Military Services Museum, Maldon Essex. ©Lady Priscilla Etienne (2020).

Hallsville School Plague P38-39 Hallsville School Uncovered, Facebook.com

Propaganda Posters. P40-41), Combined Military Services Museum. Maldon Essex. ©Lady Priscilla Etienne (2020).

South Hallsville School P59 Top, WW2talk.com, Bottom, Advertiser Newspapers.

Winston Churchill Day Morning After Bomb, P60, Top. Hallsville School. P60 Bottom, Advertiser Newspapers.

Children Sitting, P61 Top, Family In Anderson Shelter Bottom, Advertiser Newspapers.

Aldwych Station P62 Top Flashbak.com Women Knitting, Bottom. Flashbak.com.

Bombed Hospital P63 Top, Flashbak.com, Bottom Woman Hanging Washing, Bottom Flashbak.com.
ARP Wardens P64 Flashbak.com, P65 Breakfast in Anderson Shelter, Flashbak.com.
Bombed High-street, P66 Top, Flashbak.com, Bottom Nurses with Babies.

Bombed St Paul's Cathedral Priest, P67Top,Flashbak.com, Bottom Queen and King George.
Christmas Underground Shelter, P68 ©Leonard.R.Dailymail Newspapers.
Underground family, P69 Flashbak.com.
Cupboard Shelter at nursery, P70 Telegraph Newspapers.
Hospital Nurses, P71, All Posters.com/Pinterest.co.UK.
London News Front Cover, P72. ©Granger/Fineartamerica/Pinterest.co.uk.
Dustman, P73, Flashbak.com
Dig For Victory, P74, Telegraph Newspapers.
Daily Life House. P75 .Pinterest.co.UK.
Girl Wounded, P76. Pinterest.co.UK
Sir John Anderson P80, RGShistory.word-press.com/tillers2214

CONTENTS

Introduction — 11

Olley — 14

Marigold — 19

Alfred — 26

Pat & Emily — 33

Short Family Reports — 44

Miss Knowles — 56

Sir John Anderson — 78

PREFACE

The second world war began on 2 September 1940. There were many casualties and fatalities. Six years of total devastation for so many families. Children having to fend for themselves with the loss of their parents and their homes. A number of schools were bombed in the East-end. South Hallsville School was bombed in the first week of the second world war.

I was asked to become one of the administrators for a face book group that was started by Jenny Stafford called 'South Hallsville School Uncovered'. Hallsville School is situated in an area of London in which me and Jenny were born and grew up in, Custom House. Jenny had a particular interest in the story because her great-grandmother Olley Stafford had perished in the incident.

As children we all used to play in the park which is situated directly opposite the school in Agate Road. At that time in the early seventies; most of the families in the area were descendants from the late thirties, forties, and fifties.

I had seen a plaque at the school when I was young but was never really sure what it was for. My group of friends had not spoken about it with me so I did not hear any personal stories about the tragic events that unfolded there.

It was the largest mass death of civilians in this country of the second world war..

Communities pulled together, particularly the working class and sharing with your neighbours was instrumental to survival. Lots of gardens had air raid shelters in them, mine included. Although when the seventies arrived some of them were removed to make way for new garden landscape projects. Air raid shelters were available in different locations dotted around the whole of the U.K. there are still many around.

So many people could have survived if they had stayed at home and went to their own air raid shelters. The people who left home go to Hallsville School trusted the advice they were given, but would certainly not have imagined the aftermath of the bombing and the way it was handled.

The chapters contained within the book are titled with the names of some of the victims.

The area was called Canning Town after the first viceroy of India, The 1st Earl Charles John Canning. He was an English Statesmen who acquired his role after the transfer of power from the East India Company to the crown of Queen Victoria in 1858, after the rebellion was crushed.

Jenny Staffords purpose for starting the group is to get the truth out for the negligence, concealing the number of deaths and the manner in which the victims not recoverd were buried.

Charles John Canning
1st Viceroy of India

OLLEY

On 7th September 1940, another day of trying to cope with war was just like the difficult years before. Casualties were beginning to accumulate quickly. London had already suffered the hardships and heartbreaks of the first world war, there had been a complete change in lifestyles. People had to get used to carrying gas masks again. Curfews had returned and were largely followed. It didn't take long for Londoners to resume rules and certain requirements. In the local area the community was small and it was easy and natural for neighbours to support each other. The distance between the two areas Custom House and Canning town were pretty close with the local park serving as a pleasant alleyway to the school gates at Agate Road.

There was news of the deadly and imminent attack and families were advised to go to one of the local schools which had a large basement, the school was South Hallsville School. Large buildings such as the local schools made likely targets because they were in Central areas which would undoubtedly cause widespread damage and destruction.
In most gardens people had their own air raid shelters these were solid and reliable most of the time. It would seem that it was thought better for the local community to

be kept together rather on be kept within their own households. Everyone in the surrounding area were told to go to Hallsville School and take shelter in the basement. With doubts in some of their minds and escalating fear, a large number of families made their way to the school taking very little of their possessions with them. By the time everyone was assembled and into the basement it was clear that some members of families were missing. There wasn't enough time to locate the missing members. Anxiety levels were high for all those waiting; for their families to get word of where they were and for the sound of air bombers to approach the building, not being able to choose between which one they would rather hear first.
Over the next three days people were arriving to find their families but there was still no word from local authorities as to how long they would be there.

The bombs hit on 10th September bringing total devastation. The impact ripped through the school and half of the building fell into the basement killing and seriously injuring the people inside, there were still people arriving so they were extra hands to help with the rescue effort. Wardens were there to help alongside the frantic families witnessing it.
    The story that was circulayed was a different version of events that the local community recounted.

There were reports in the news that the buses intended for evacuation from the area went to Camden Town instead of Canning Town. There were a number of radio controllers working shifts and around the clock throughout the war. Mistakes could happen through fear, fatigue, and pressure. There was a definite delay in executing a plan of action, particularly when there were warnings of imminent bombing in the area.

Olley was the mother of George. After the bombing George would not talk about it to anyone but he had a strong hatred for Winston Churchill. He sadly had the task of identifying his mother and sister. He joined other families at the local swimming baths at Romford Road, East London to make identifications. George did not recognise his mother at first because he walked straight past her, the dust and debris from the attack had left masses of white dust in her usual raven black hair. Olley could only be identified by her ring as her body condition had changed too.

After the bomb had hit it came to light that there wasn't a mistake with locations to where the evacuation buses were headed. It was originally circulated that the radio operators taking instructions where to deploy evacuation buses, had made an error. Many were led to believe that the location of Canning Town was given as Camden Town. But it seems there were no operators manning the phones to take the instructions during that weekend.

On Olley's death certificate the cause of death was stated as 'Due to war operations'.

OLLEY STAFFORD
LOUISA STANNARD
IRENE STANNARD
GEORGE WILLIAM STREETON
ALICE SUTTON
FRANK WILLIAM JAMES SWIFT
ROBERT JAMES TAYLOR
WILLIAM GEORGE THOMPSON
WALTER A TOMLINSON
ISOBELLA E TOMLINSON

Afterword

Winston Churchill became Prime Minister on the day of the Hallsviile School bombing 10th September 1940. He took over from Neville Chamberlain. The favourite at the time was Lord Halifax, regarded by many as solid and reliable. Churchill had forty years of experience but was regarded to be a warmonger and opportunist, a sure loose cannon. Chamberlain resigned and it was hoped that Halifax would step into the role but he declined. Churchill was then appointed. There was a lot of talk in government at the time of Churchill's state of mind, how he had a strong urge to fight and partly the reason was that his nephew had already spent a month in captivity in Narvik Norway.

Within a couple of days of the bombing Winston Churchill went to Hallsville school. This would have been a good opportunity for him to search his mixed feelings that he had towards his nephews plight and firstly think of the harrowing experience that the community had to bear. Misconduct was disguised as tactics. Concealing the truth was a way of escaping responsibility and duty to support the families of the soldiers who physically fought to win. Olleys's son George went on to have a family of his own, and fathered thirteen children. George was never the same after the bombing, and his working life was greatly affected.

MARIGOLD

I should start Marigolds' story by telling you that she is not too fond of her name, she never was. At the end of our conversation she tells the story of how she thinks she came to have her name. Mary was three-years-old at the time off the bombing and got the account of her story from her dad Alec, who was in the Navy and at sea. Her mother and grandmother both died in the bombing. Alec was not told about the bombing until he returned home. He was initially told that he had lost all his family when in fact, there had been some separation. Mary's two older sisters were taken to Devon with the first coaches for evacuation.
The second coaches for mothers and babies never arrived. The explosion left Mary buried in the rubble for a couple of days. Mary's brother Tom bore the blast and was blown out of the school into the playground and was dug out soon after because he managed to get one arm free to wave for rescue from beneath the rubble. He was fourteen years old. Mary's mum was Emily, here's was the second name on the list of fatalities and Mary's was the third, at this point it was not known that she was alive. Mary's little sister was around the sixth person on the list, when in fact she too survived because Mary shielded her from the blast. Mary's injuries were extensive, she suffered a fractured skull, fractured vertebrae in her spine.

Her legs were damaged internally and left her with a lot of surface scars.

As soon as Tom received medical attention and was safe to leave hospital, he returned to the family home at Martindale Road but it had been completely destroyed. So he began a life on the road looking for permanent work and odd jobs anywhere he could. He had landed some work gardening for a woman , and during his break he went to get fish and chips. The newspaper his dinner was wrapped in had a photo of Mary and his baby sister Rosemary in it. He told the lady who employed him what he has seen and that they were alive. The woman phoned The Daily Mirror newspaper and they saw it as another great story to add to their growing 'Reunited Again' campaign. They had been visiting hospitals and been taking pictures of survivors for the paper to help identify them. A journalist and photographer arranged to take Tom to the hospital. When they arrived, Tom was instructed to walk down the ward but not to call Mary's name. They wanted to see if she would recognise him. Tom began the slow walk scanning the ward with this eyes from left to right. Mary had been brought into the hospital with her baby sister Rosemary and they were kept together despite th fact that Mary was in a coma and medical staff were not certain they were related. Now Mary was awake and the day Mary saw her brother looking around she called him by his name; 'Tom, our Tom!'. The photographer rushed forward and started taking pictures of the joy, tears and laughter from both of them. Mary's father Alec had arrived at the hospital soon after and they were all back together. It was great news for Alec knowing that most of his family had indeed survived. When hospital staff saw Mary responding to the baby once awake, and then playing with her, they knew then they must be sisters but it wasn't confirmed until Mary's brother then father turned up. Mary kept telling the staff that the baby was hers.

When Mary was released from the hospital, a shift to many different homes began. Mary was separated from Rosemary and they never lived together again. Mary's two older sisters came back from Devon after the war and she was placed with them in a foster home. She wasn't told the girls were her sisters. After being in the foster home for a while her dad Alec took her to his mum to look after Mary while he went to try and get more work on another boat. He couldn't find work and went back to his mum to try and negotiate Mary's stay because he didn't have any money to contribute to her needs. During this time, if there was no money to support a child the workhouse was the next option for homeless and disadvantaged mothers and children. Sadly Mary's grandmother took her to Livington and put her in a workhouse. After a short while Alec asked his sister (Mary's aunt) to get her out.

Mary grew up not really knowing anything about her family. At seventeen Mary want to get married to her sweetheart Charlie but she had to get proof that her parents were deceased. She went to her local registry office at West Ham Lane in east London. Once her name was given a search for her identity should have brought up her details, instead it produced a death certificate, along with her sisters. Mary had been surprised to learn that she had been registered dead for the past fourteen years dating back to her age at the time of the bombing. A line was drawn with a pen on the death certificate, right in front of Mary. The registrar wrote something on it, perhaps the word 'alive' or 'not deceased'. She was offered a copy of the inaccurate death certificate but Mary refused it. She wishes now that she had kept it as one of her personal keepsakes. The registrar then asked Mary what she should put on her sisters. Mary knew she was alive because she had heard about her well being but never saw her again either. A monument was erected and for years Mary along with other families were putting flowers there. Some years later Mary moved away from the area, it was then Mary's husband told her that her mum wasn't at the school site. There were still people and some remains left at the school but Mary's mother and grandmother were taken out. Mary never discovered where her mother and grandmother were buried. Mary suffered for many years after the bombing, She had terrible nightmares and recalls the peculiar dreams she used to have where she would see big balls falling from the sky. Some were rough and some were smooth, she remembers how scared she felt when she saw the smooth ones, she began to like the rough ones as they would appear to be less dangerous.

An experience like this can take a long time to work through, come to terms with and accept. The site of the bombing has never been built on because of the people still remaining there. It can't be built on for one hundred years. This year is the eighty year anniversary of the bombing. For some time afterwards Mary's dad Alec would show the scars on her legs whenever they were in friends company, he would say; "Look, she'll take that to her grave with her".

By Mary's reckoning the last twenty years have been completely and truly happy. Mary is eighty two now, and has three daughters, one of whom lives just around the corner. She survived all her siblings despite everything she has been through and is still very active and able.
I asked Mary how she is coping in the Corona Virus pandemic and she said; 'Well Hitler never got me, so I'm not gonna let that kill me'.

Afterword

For a child so young to have lost so much stability all at once is truly upsetting. Major family members; mothers, fathers and grandparents heads of families were gone in an instant. There was a lot of practical thinking among people during war time, learning how to make the smallest amounts stretch as fare as possible and with that came a harshness with no time to dwell on sadness but to get on with the jobs in hand. It was felt there was no time to ponder the misfortunes of so many.
The children were the worst casualties of the war with few familiar faces to welcome them back at the end, they had to re-settle with relatives or spend their childhood living with carer's or guardians.

Imagine being so badly injured and having to recover without either of your parents holding your hand when you become conscious. This would have been scary and really confusing. Children rightly felt insecure and most certainly neglected in some cases. It took many years for Mariglold to overcome these feelings and be able to re-build her life fully.

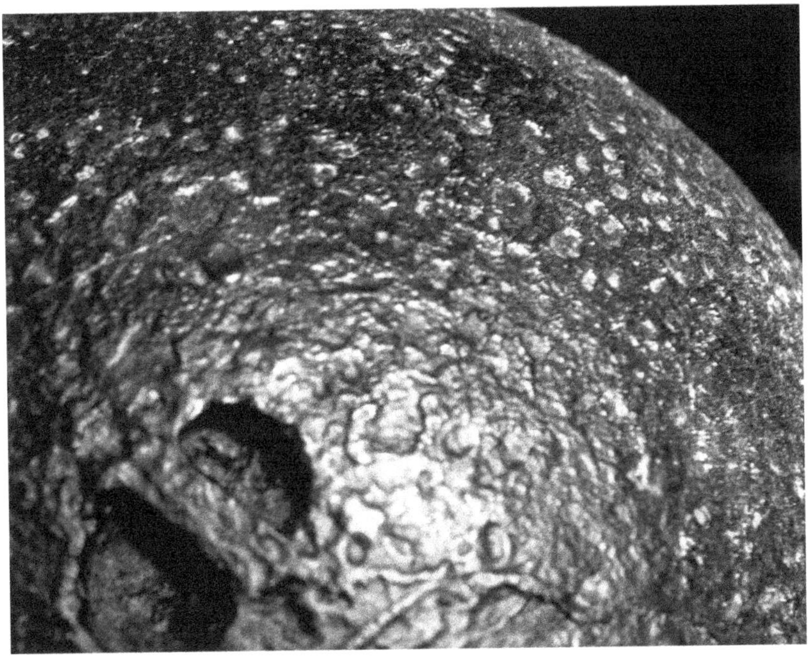

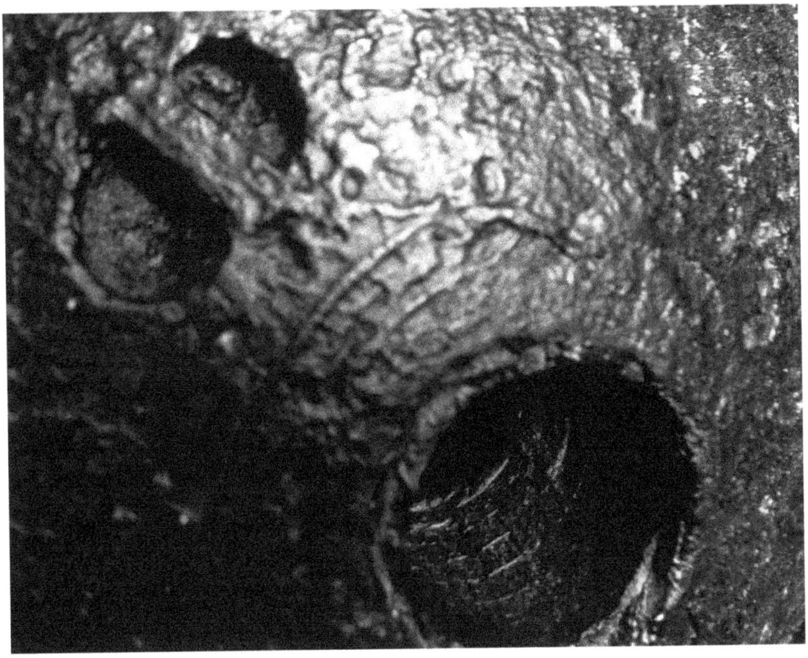

Alfred

Alfred was an A.R.P. Warden, a role that was set by the government and delivered by each local authority, their job was to protect civilians from the danger of air raids and to patrol the streets during black out and make sure no light was visible.
As there were quite a few air raid warnings at staggered times a warden would make sure that shelters were taking civilians in and keeping them safe until they could be evacuated and sent to safer areas.

Albert had received instructions to go to Hallsville School to open up a rest centre for the community there were a group of women from the W.V.S (Women's Voluntary Service), they were still setting up when the victims began to arrive many were bombed out and made homeless. There was a few hours respite once the all clear was given on the Saturday morning and the time was used to clear up the mess in the surrounding area. Just after lunchtime the raiders were back and the next few hours were worse than the night before, many more were killed and injured and more homes were lost. The gas and electricity were disconnected and the water began to run inconsistently. When the all clear was sounded on the Saturday evening the situation was clearly desperate. The district and Post Wardens were sent to Hallsvillle School and Albert discussed the situation with them.

It was decided that an urgent message be sent to the control room, they asked for a fleet of buses or any sort of transport to get everyone out before nightfall. There was a long wait in vain, because the buses never arrived. The air raid continued from Saturday night through to Sunday, with each bomb that fell a few more were added to the swelling numbers. At around eight on the Monday evening they were preparing for another ordeal that would last throughout the night when quite suddenly, the warning siren sounded.Everyone was surprised as it came much earlier than usual. By now the rest centre was crammed with people, this raid was different though, the bombs were fewer in number but they were heavier and bigger. The ARP Wardens called them heavy calibre bombs but civilians called them aerial torpedo's. The first one that fell seemed to be very close but in fact it was several streets away, as more came down one after another they seemed to be getting nearer and nearer and soon everyone began to think the next one would hit them. There were only two wardens left on duty in the school, a young girl named Vicky and Albert they were both part time wardens. They stationed themselves one each end of the shelter and they kept contact with each other by periodically moving down the length of the corridor and exchanging notes but as time went on this was getting increasingly difficult.

It was nearing two thirty in the morning, Albert had not seen or heard from his colleague Vicky for over half an hour he knew it was nearly time to check on her and take notes. He tried to get through the crowds but realised it was hopeless but then he had a better idea, he decided to come out of the school at his end to make a run for it across the playground, then go in at the other need. He became aware that Vicky had somehow managed to scramble through and as he went out of the door she arrived at his end. Albert was just about to dash to the other end when he heard a whistling through the air, he threw himself down flat and then came a terrific crunch sound. As he lifted his eyes he saw one half of the school disappear in a cloud of smoke and dust, his first thought was for young Vicky but as he picked himself up she came running out calling his name.

Hallsville School itself was a quite formidable building, it consisted of two floors and a flat roof of re-enforced concrete asphalt which formed an elevated playground for the older boys of the school. Generally the building was a very good air raid shelter like other schools had in the area but with a direct hit it became a death trap. I knew that it might be some time before we would get help, however the warden post was almost within sight of the school so Albert knew it would not be necessary to report the incident. He grabbed hold of the next person he saw and shouted; 'Run like hell to the police station and tell them what's happened'!

Faith in the police was not very strong during war time but according to Albert they came up tops on this occasion, as did the suddenly present Home Guard Officer. He often wondered who he was because he disappeared as quickly as he came when the rescue task was completed. Very soon the scene was a hive of activity and joining the rescue were policemen, St John's Ambulance, firemen from the local station and many more emergency services. They thought nothing of their own safety and were only concerned with helping others they were all there. The obvious absentees were the selfish few who put their safety first. The injured on ground level were accessible for treatment but for the people who were trapped there was not much that could be done but to desperately scratch and scrape at the tons of concrete made with steel girders.

Daylight was coming, it was Monday at seven in the morning. A message had already been sent to control to cancel the buses and send morgue vans and ambulances.

A small group of people were standing on the edge of the crater the bomb made, near Albert was Councillor Paten the staff officer in charge of public shelters. As they stood there he lifted his head to the sky and with tears streaming done his face he said;

'My god, my god this should have never happened'. There was another warden present much older than Albert thought to be a tyrant and very outspoken. He swung around with some force and grabbed the councillor by the arm saying: 'And it wouldn't have happened either if you and your mates hadn't buggered off down the country for the weekend'.

The clearing of the area would continue. The official number of people killed was around eighty or ninety but that did not allow for the ones who were never found. Only the German air raid squad The Luftwaffe can be held responsible for the bomb that hit the school but many people lost their lives because of those who failed in their responsibilities to the civilian.

At the end of the war the ARP was renamed the Civil Defence then stood down but it was revived again in the nineteen fifties and named The Civil Defence Corps.

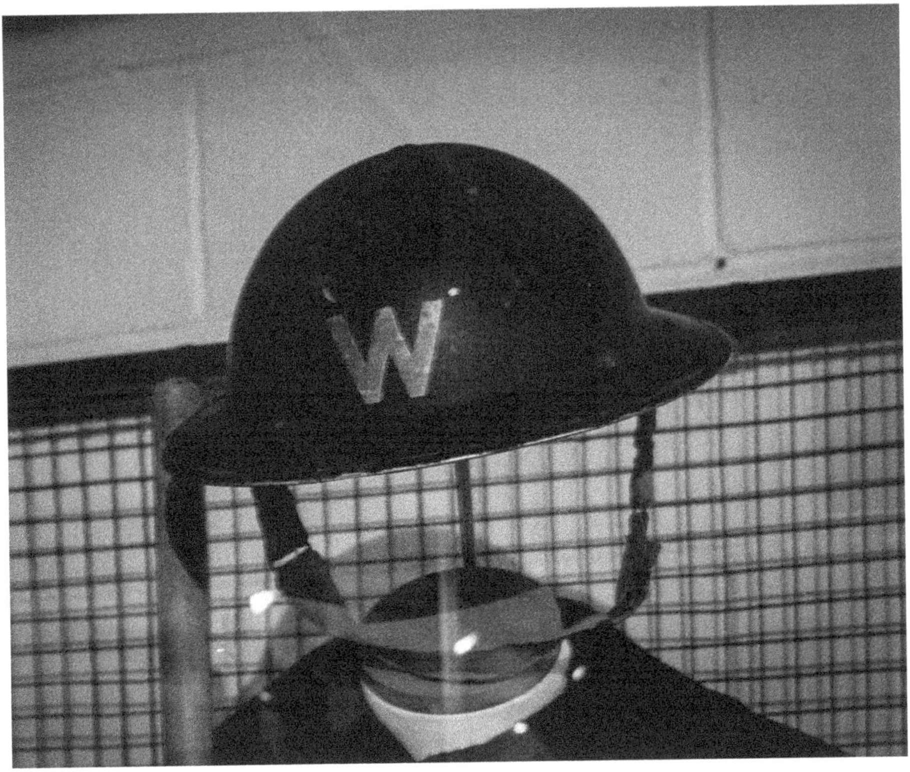
W

Afterword

Albert's account of the story took me there; to the sounds, smells and atmosphere. He had a strong sense of duty and really sound organisational skills. He did everything expected of him but his anger was all too apparent, he did his utmost to keep civilians as safe as possible. For many of the ARP wardens, this was the goal throughout the world wars but this level of negligence was never an expected part of it.

Albert felt strongly enough to record all of the events in detail and they have been kept for many of years. Who did he hope would read them in the future?

Pat & Emily

Pat and Emily were at Hallsville School that fateful day because Emily went looking for her mother to tell her they had sold their shop. When they got there Emily s' mother had gone out the other side of the building and as they went in the school was hit. Emily's two children Pat and Sheila were instantly orphaned. Emily's mother was known as granny mac. Sheila was taken to a large house where she was told by officials that her parents had been killed, naturally she cried but was smacked for crying by a woman who would be taking over guardianship for her, she was seven-years-old. Granny Mac sent dresses for Sheila to wear but she never wore them because they were packed away. To Sheila it looked like there wasn't going to be anything nice for her, she wanted to have a part of the life she had before the bombing and she knew she would need some of her own money to this. She became a 'ratter'. This involved catching rats killing them and cutting their tails off to return them to whomever hired the ratter. There was payment given for every rat killed.

Pat was evacuated to Devon when his mother was killed but Emily stayed just outside the borough and was taken to a large house with wealthy occupants but she was desperately unhappy there despite the house being glorious, organised and very clean. The extreme sorrow led to the decision to send Sheila to live with granny mac and one that would see Sheila flourish and find some comfort from being orphaned and separated from her brother that attributed to her immense loss.

Granny macs house at Lesley Road East London doubled as a refuge for many locals who had lost their homes, there were all manner of people living there, some of the women taking shelter were prostitutes with a few men to pay for their company it was a hive of activity which took Sheila some time to get used to. The surroundings were not luxurious or grand and there was a need for a more regular cleaning routine. Granny mac was old when her grandchildren were orphaned and she did not want the responsibility of looking after two young children, she had already brought her children up so she took Sheila and Pat to her son-in-laws side of the family. The family did not think they could give Sheila what she needed and did not think it was the best place for Sheila and suggested that she be taken to a convent for training to become a nun. Sheila and her brother Pat were left money in the event of their parents death and that money was received along with a bungalow in Maldon Essex. Both were taken from Sheila and Pat by her dads side of the family. The convent idea did not happen thankfully and Sheila was allowed to stay with granny mac where she found the majority of the east end community so much nicer and whatever gifts and possessions were given to Sheila were never taken from her again. On her eighteenth birthday it was intended that Sheila would recvieve one hundred pounds from her parents. If the interest on the amount had been left to accumulate the amount would have been considerably higher but granny mac had no choice other than to use the interest to help support Sheila. Everyone drunk during the times to calm and settle the nerves and lift spirits through incredibly stressful times. It was a culture shock for Sheila to be in the midst of a working class community and experience first hand the struggles they all faced. The best thing for Sheila was that at granny macs house she was shown love, warmth and compassion.

Granny mac was a small woman of four foot ten with long hair plaited all the way down her back and she had tattoos. She was once married to a man who had a daughter but after a time they split and he left her but did not take his daughter who had a disability because she couldn't talk properly, her name was Annie. Granny macs demise came as a result of getting drunk in her local pub The Spanish Steps with her friend Mrs Brewster. She was coming out and was drunk, she fell and her friend fell on top of her so broke her hip, soon after this granny mac died.

Children who were left without parents were imposed on extended family members and sometimes friends this would happen whether the children were wanted or not. Evacuations had to go ahead because the safety of the children, the next generation was paramount a large death toll of children was not an option. The circumstances of Sheila's life made her quite hard, her brother Pat went to New Zealand when he came of age with the Merchant Navy and settled there. Sheila went on to fall in love and marry and by chance she married back into a wealthy family so her former life of stability as a young child was regained, she had five children and lived a full and very happy life. When one of her daughters, Raewyne turned twenty one it was arranged for her brother Pat to attend the party. It was to be a surprise and she had absolutely no idea he was coming. When he entered the hall and Sheila saw him she cried uncontrollably, it was the first time she had seen him since they were separated as evacuees.

Afterword

I know how important war children were, protection was key for future generations to survive. I understand the implications for economy and for rehabilitation. Equally important was the emotional and psychological state of these children. There were more children separated from their siblings than not, a continued relationship with their siblings was hardly ever an option. There doesn't seem to be reasonable enough explanations for this, particularly for the children who went to wealthy families. Emotional scars from this treatment has left afflictions that spanned over many years.

To steal from some of the people who died is an act of desperation, greed, opportunity and dishonesty. As victims of war grew in numbers many civilians were forced to think on their feet and find their way in the world to survive. There were lots of people suddenly becoming guardians to their families children with no time to prepare practically or financially, some didn't want the responsibility this is true but some just couldn't cope with the sudden change to their life and household. Workhouses were the next option for countless people. There could not have been much piece of mind for those who had to make such unwanted hard decisions, with plenty of bedsheets over disturbed because countless sleeps were less than restful.

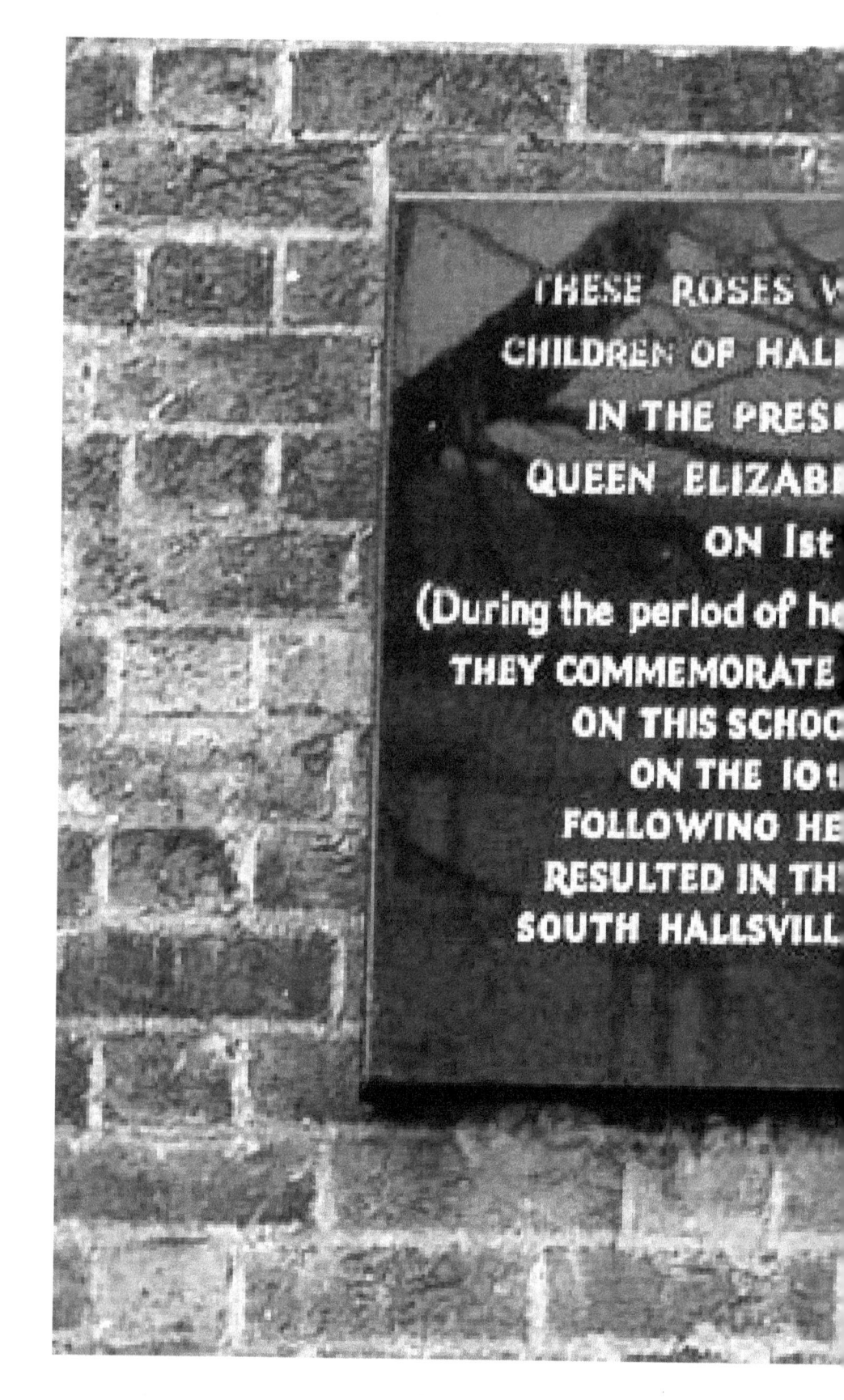

THESE ROSES W[...]
CHILDREN OF HAL[...]
IN THE PRES[...]
QUEEN ELIZAB[...]
ON 1st [...]
(During the period of he[...]
THEY COMMEMORATE [...]
ON THIS SCHOO[...]
ON THE 10t[...]
FOLLOWING HE[...]
RESULTED IN TH[...]
SOUTH HALLSVILL[...]

...PLANTED BY THE
... PRIMARY SCHOOL
... OF HER MAJESTY
... HE QUEEN MOTHER
... JST 1990.
... h Birthday celebrations)
... WHO LOST THEIR LIVES
... 50 YEARS AGO
... TEMBER 1940
... BOMBING WHICH
... STRUCTION OF THE
... OOL, AGATE STREET.

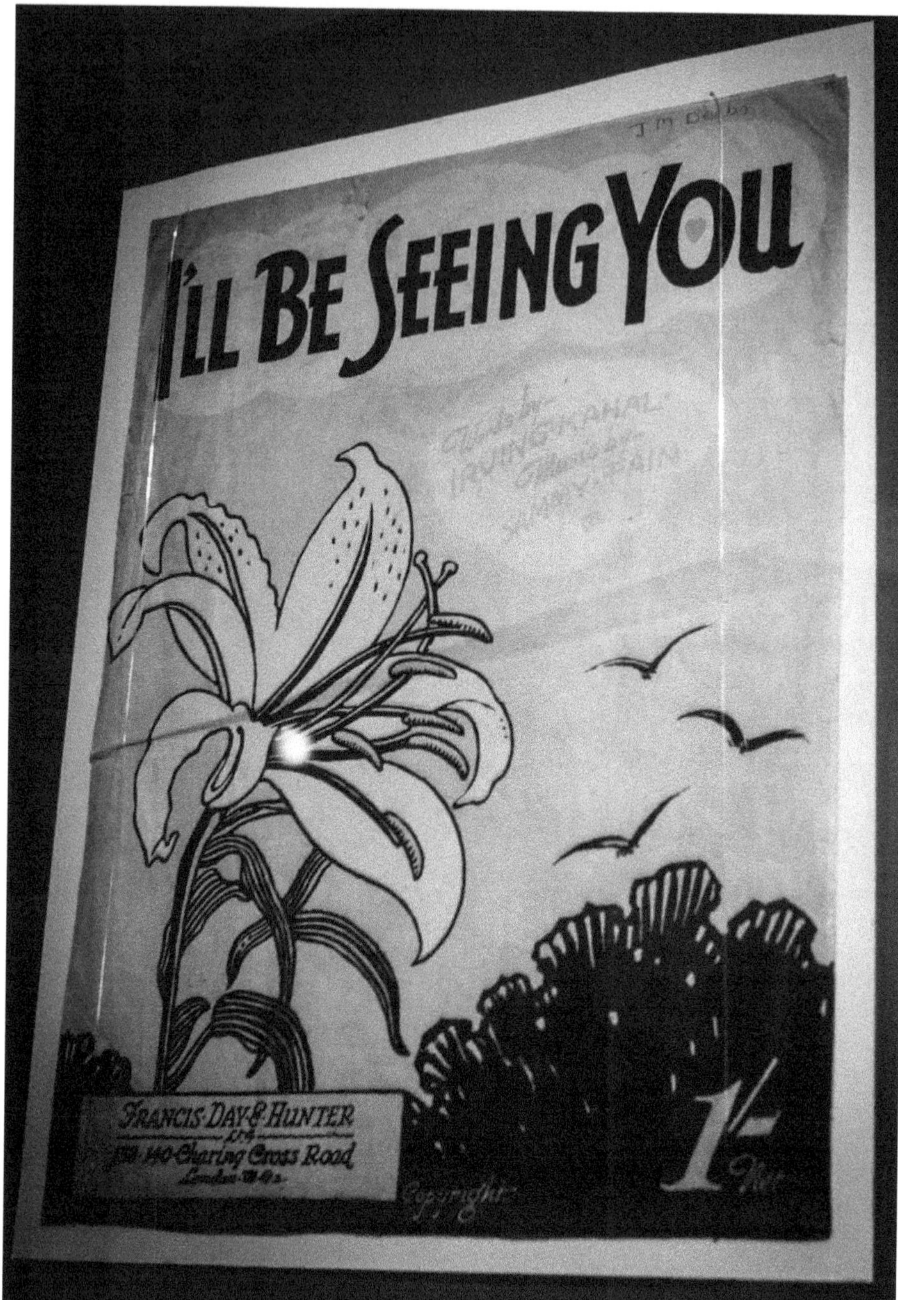
I'LL BE SEEING YOU
FRANCIS, DAY & HUNTER
Copyright
1/- Net

There'll always be an England
by
ROSS PARKER &
HUGHIE CHARLES
1/-
NET

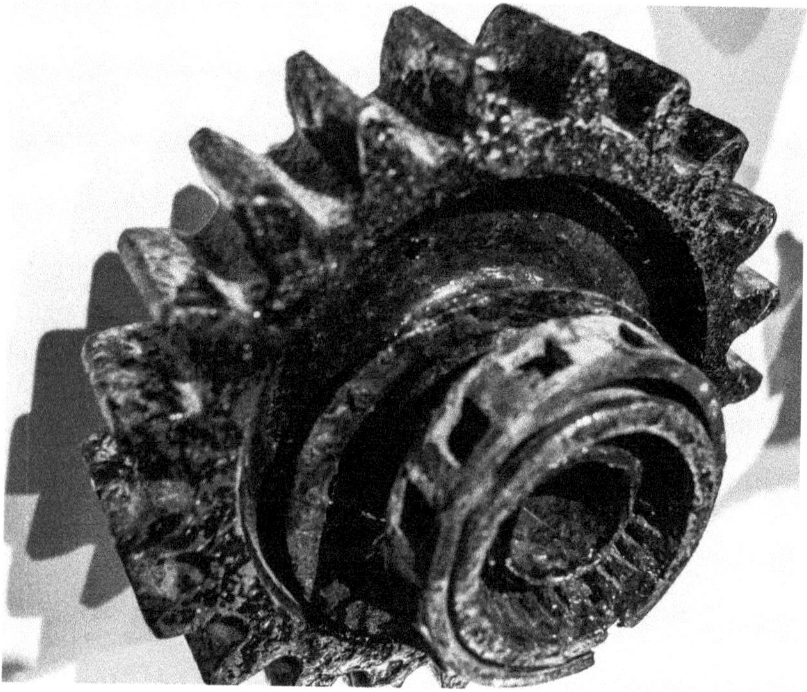

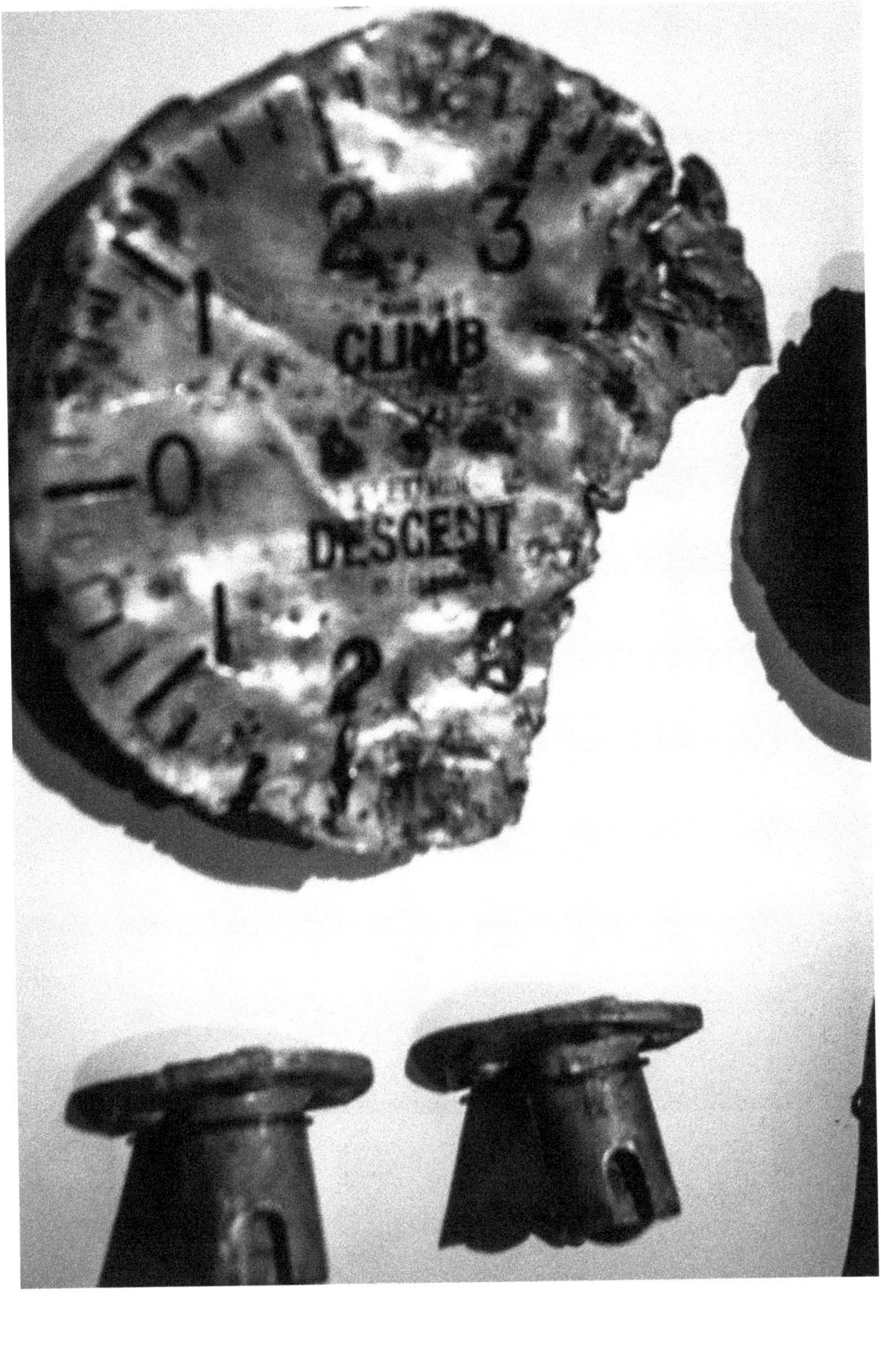
2
3
1
CLIMB
0
DESCENT
1

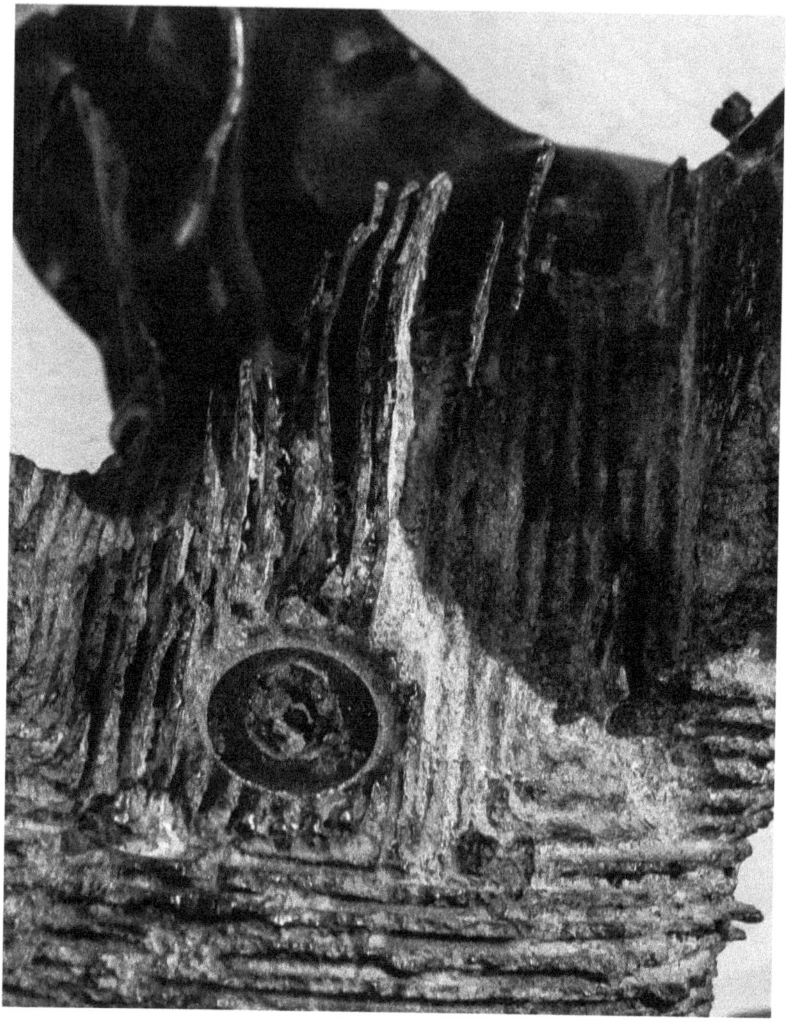

HOME OFFICE
THE PROTECTION OF YOUR HOME AGAINST AIR RAIDS
READ THIS BOOK THROUGH
THEN
KEEP IT CAREFULLY
AIR RAID PRE
DIRECTI
FOR THE ERECTION
OF THE GALVANISE
STEEL SHE

Short Family Reports

Ivy

Ivy lived at 32 Brixham Road, she was on her way to the school with her sisters Jean and Lucy but they realised they had forgotten something at home and ran back. On the way back to school Lucy spotted the German plane and could see the pilots head as the plane was so low. Ivy and Jean survived without any harm but Lucy was permanently deafened by the blast along with other injuries. She was never fully well after the bombing and died at forty two years.

Sue

Sue's' grandparents lived in the roads that were bombed they always told her the story of Hallsville. 'My grandfathers family, the Browrings were dispersed through the country after this bombing but some of them simply disappeared with no trace or record. I feel sure they are amongst the dead in that playground but they tale was always of my grandfathers family. My great grandmother Jane along with her two youngest children sheltered in the school for the first three days, they got really fed up and decided to walk across town to my grandmothers house near the Boleyn East Ham, they left two hours before the bomb fell'.

Eliza

Eliza lived in nearby Lansdowne Road with her daughter. Her son Tim had died five years earlier at nineteen years from throat cancer and nine years before that her husband died. On the day of the bombing they were late getting to the school and because it was full they were refused entry. Eliza knew a local policeman and he suggested they stay in a police cell in the nearby police station, they both survived.

Alexandra

Alexandra's father also had to go to the Romford Road swimming baths to identify his family, he hated Churchill and called him a warmonger. Alexandra's mother and family were waiting in a queue for the evacuation buses, an older couple in front of them suddenly remembered they had left their canary back in another school called Fredrick Street. Her mother went back to get the canary for the couple but when she returned the buses had left, she got on the next one having no idea where her family had gone.'The driver had intended to drop people off at the side of the road, he dropped my mother off at Epping in Essex where she eventually found her family sitting outdoors around an open fire. They lived like that for several days before being offered sanctuary by the people of Epping'.

Helen

Helen worked at Hallsville school in the later years. 'I was told how the children were killed by bombs in world war two. Father Moore and Father Goose from nearby St Luke's Church came into school to talk to the children and staff about the past tragedy. I was not told initially how many were buried, only that some were buried alive. It was decided to begin to raise funds for a memorial to be erected which eventually happened'.

Debbie

'My uncle Pat went to school there at the time. When the bomb dropped I know my granddad helped digging with his bare hands for four days but he would never talk about it in any detail'.

Darren

'My great nan Rose was at the school an hour before the bombing but her mother had a feeling that she shouldn't be there and decided to go and collect her, that gut instinct was right. She went on to have children of her own and lived long enough to see my eldest, making her a great grandmother'.

Deb

'My nan and her family were also sheltering at the school but she was overcome by a great sense of foreboding so they moved to seek shelter beneath the arches near Tidal basin, lucky escape'!

Jean

Jean learned of the bombing because of the BBC documentary, she discovered a bomb was dropped outside number eight Martindale Road, the people living in the street were evacuated to the school to shelter. Her great uncle, aunt and two cousins lived at number ten but went to the school to shelter. 'They were all killed when the school was hit, my dad was twenty one years old and in the army abroad, he didn't know about his uncle and family until the war ended'.

Chrissy

'I had some friends named Jim and Nell they lived on the fifth floor of Rowland Court, they always talked about the tragedy and the government cover up because Nell was just a baby and one of the few to survive but she was left alone in the world as her entire family perished, most unrecorded but still entombed there'.

Nancy

'My granddad brother Jimmy died there that day he was helping people who had been bombed out, he was nineteen years old'.

Bill

'My mother was in that school the night it got bombed, she was on one side of the hall and got moved to the other side. She lost a lot of her classmates that day and the blast left her with deafness in one ear. Her class were singing We'll Meet Again when the bomb hit, she could never listen to that song again afterwards. The nightmare stayed with her all her life'.

Vera

'After the war there was hardly a school left in Canning Town, the ones that were left had damage and were all overcrowded which meant different ages were taught together'.

Josie

'I can't get what happened in 1940 at my old school out of my mind. I can't believe I went there for four years and never knew the history of what was below my feet'.

Eileen

There is a memorial plaque within the grounds of the infant school. The queen mother would visit the school from time to time to commemorate the people killed'.

Jean

'My mum and her sister who had twin girls were supposed to go to the school to wait to be evacuated but there wasn't enough room for them all and my mum wouldn't leave them, she always said the number of casualties was wrong she knew that hundreds had been killed. When a national newspaper published details I was horrified, I was relieved that my mum had already passed away I think she would have been absolutely devastated to learn the truth. So much heartache and suffering is difficult to imagine'.

Paul

'My mother-in-law Nancy survived the bombing she was pulled out from the rubble after three days and thought it was angels taking her to heaven. Both her parents died, her fathers death certificate was dated as just September I assume the reason was because of a cover-up. Her mother died in hospital a few hours after Nancy was rescued without knowing that her daughter had been saved'.

Joan

'I was ten years old when the war started and sixteen when it finished. We lived in the area that was bombed. On the right of us was a large factory which produced paper and in front of us was Hallsville School which I used to attend. It was closed at the time because most of the children had been sent away to the country but my parents didn't want us to go. The sirens used to sound about nine o clock in the evening and we would go into the shelter in the garden. When the all clear was sound early the next morning we went back to our beds to try and get some sleep. One night my mother didn't feel safe in the shelter, so we went across to the school which had loads of people staying in there as they had lost their homes. My mother still didn't feel safe and did not want to go back there the next night, so we went to a shelter in a park.
Sadly the school was bombed that night and lots of people died, we were very lucky that we hadn't gone back there that night. It was a very frightening time as the enemy used bombs that whistled; my mother used to put a cover over our heads so it would dull the sound of the bombs. The night that we stayed in the park was the night our home was bombed, all that remained was a massive hole where the houses had been. I am so very proud of where I lived and all the people in the East end of London who were so very brave.

Roy

'I am a survivor of the Hallsville school bombing I was born in Martindale Road in 1936. We were told the school was a point to get buses to be transported to somewhere? The buses did not arrive so we bunked down in a corridor I was with my father. My mother, sister and baby brother went elsewhere. My mother and sister were killed and my brother was badly injured but survived with shocking scarring to his body leg and left arm, my favourite uncle Jim who was sleeping close to us was decapitated by a falling steel beam and I got a cut to the head from falling debris'.

Robert

'I was fifteen months old when my father was caught in the bombing at Hallsville School he was a RADAR man from Plymouth and was waiting with Artillery soldiers to be shipped out to India, Burma and Assam. He told of rolling his bed when the bomb struck, which protected him. There were perhaps six soldiers alive one hanging with his ankles trapped between floorboards, their biggest concern was the smell of gas, he cut through a door with his sheath knife and after some silence for rescue calls they were released. My father got two weeks compassionate leave and then shipped out, he survived and returned to Plymouth after the war with the Burma Star.

Dave

'My mother was a Fire Watch Warden she was on duty that evening being a local who lived in Cleaver Road she always maintained that the number of people who lost their lives was greater than the official figure stated. One of the worst memories that never left her was that of picking up a body of a little girl, and when my mother lifted her up the child's head, neck and arm had separated from the main torso and the rest of her body remained on the ground'.

Michael

'I have been in Brisbane since 1948, I remember my mother trying tonvisit her parents after the raid, she came home in tears saying that they had sheltered at the school and we never saw them again she believed they were in the mass grave under the ruins'.

Steve

'My mothers home was bombed on the first night of the blitz she was ten years old, she took shelter with her grandmother and siblings in the garden Anderson, there was a second family in the shelter. When the bomb destroyed the house the rubble fell on top of the shelter trapping all inside. Fortunately my grandfather had built the shelter with a second exit at the rear which enabled them to be rescued. During the next few days they took shelter in Hallsville school, my grandfather who was an ARP Warden took them all to another nearby school just an hour or so before it was hit. There seems to be no records of any bombs dropped in that area, I assume because of the cover-up'.

Afterword

I'm not convinced that there had to be a complete stop with continuing the rescue effort so as morale was not affected and the Germans were not informed of their victory. The Luftwaffe were highly skilled and trained airman they knew what they did and where to target their bombs. Morale is important even vital to continue the momentum to fight, so my question is this, Surely the fight could continue with a ban on any media coverage of the fatalities while the recovery process continued?

To bury the remaining 523 or so people where they fell, some still alive at burial is unspeakably cruel and heartless. The morale of the soldiers returning to find no trace of their family and friends would have immediately sunk their morale deep into their boots, this would have undoubtedly made their path of re-building their lives an uphill struggle forever.

Miss Knowles

Miss Knowles was a woman who lived alone and had no children, she was wealthy and was well respected in the community. She lived in a large house by a church in Martindale or possibly Chantler Road. She liked to help people the poorer working class and was very religious this gave her the persona of a priest. She would offer her services by becoming god mother to impending babies and did this multiple times. Every year Miss Knowles arranged a holiday for the locals, she would make sure the women and their children would get a very cheap or free holiday for a week. It is very likely that she got to name a lot of children because of this, she was a trusted and reliable person to know.

59

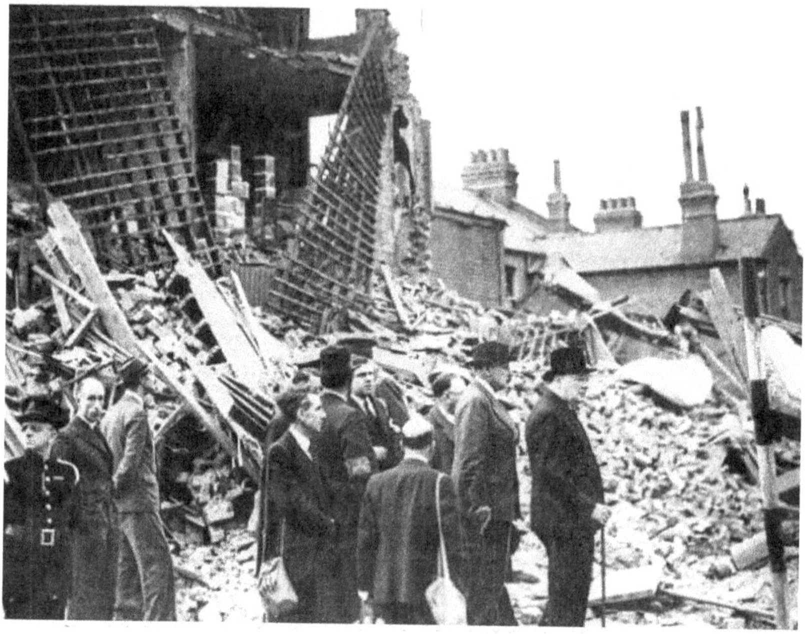

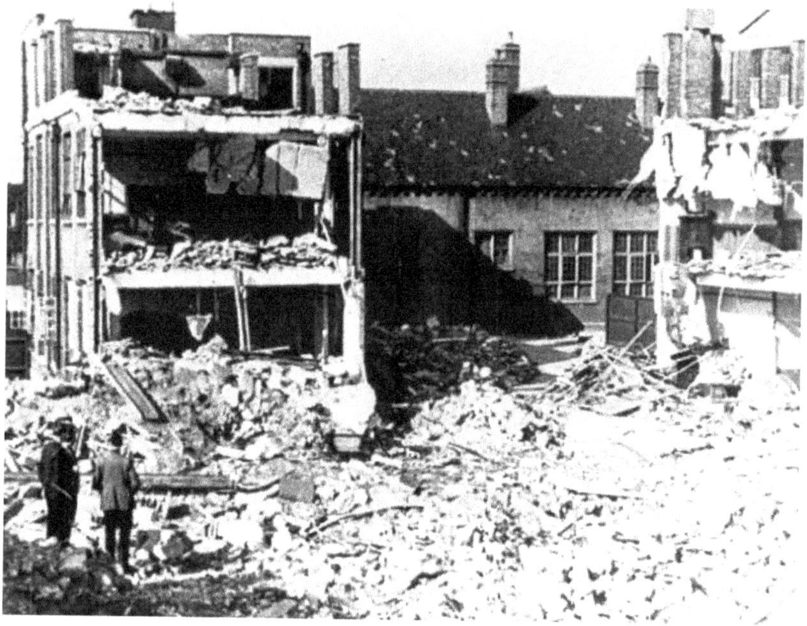

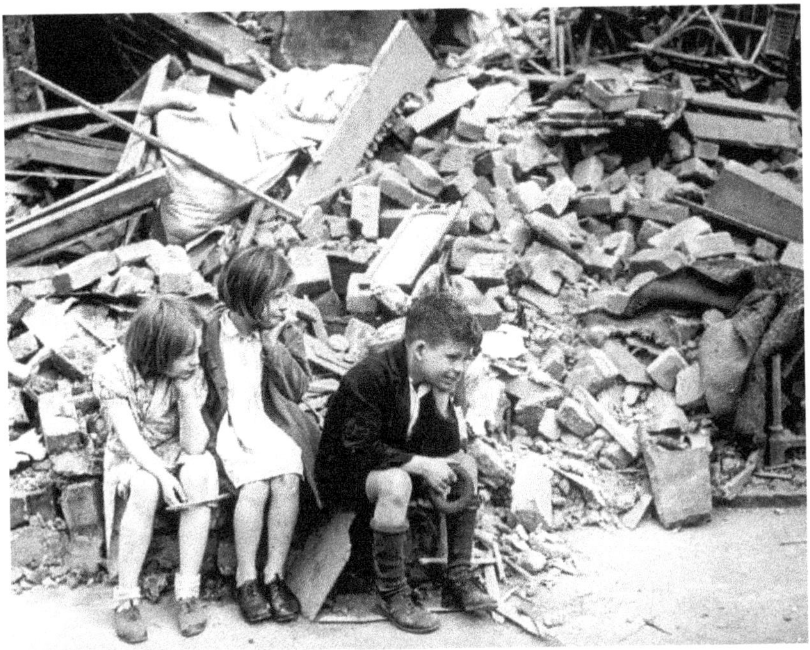

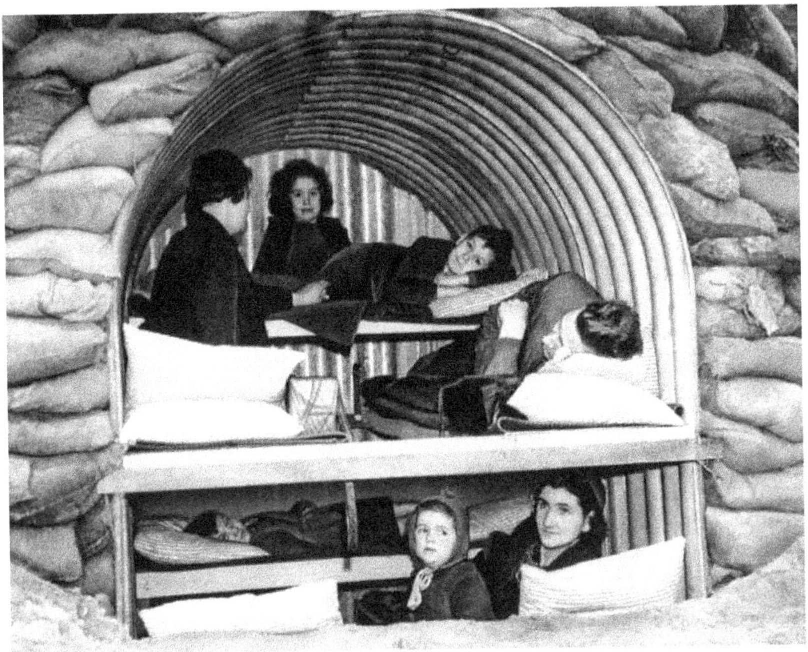

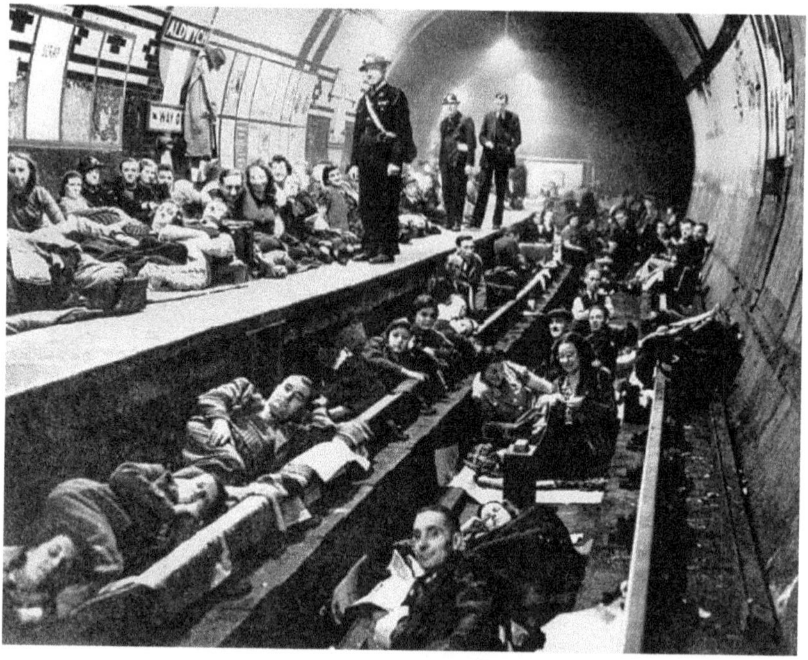

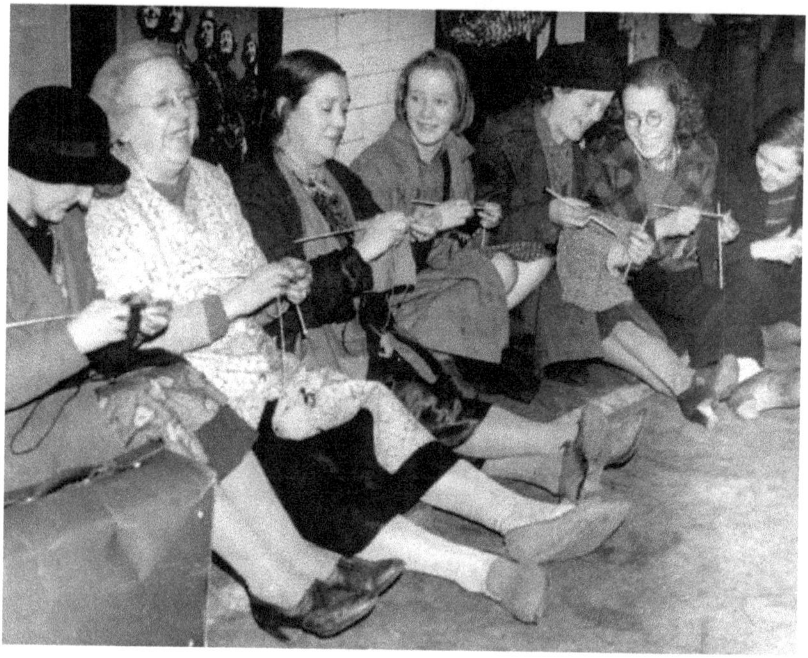

63

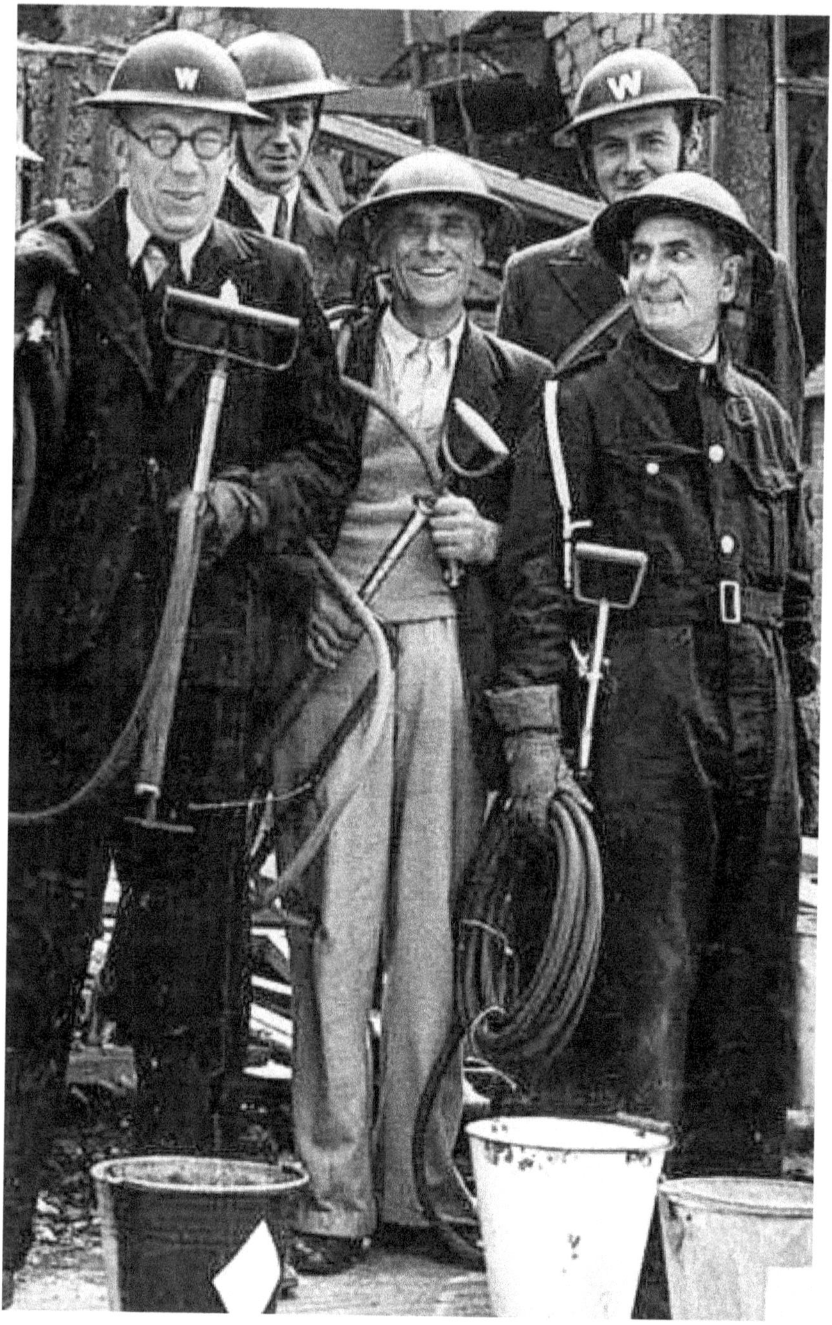
W
W

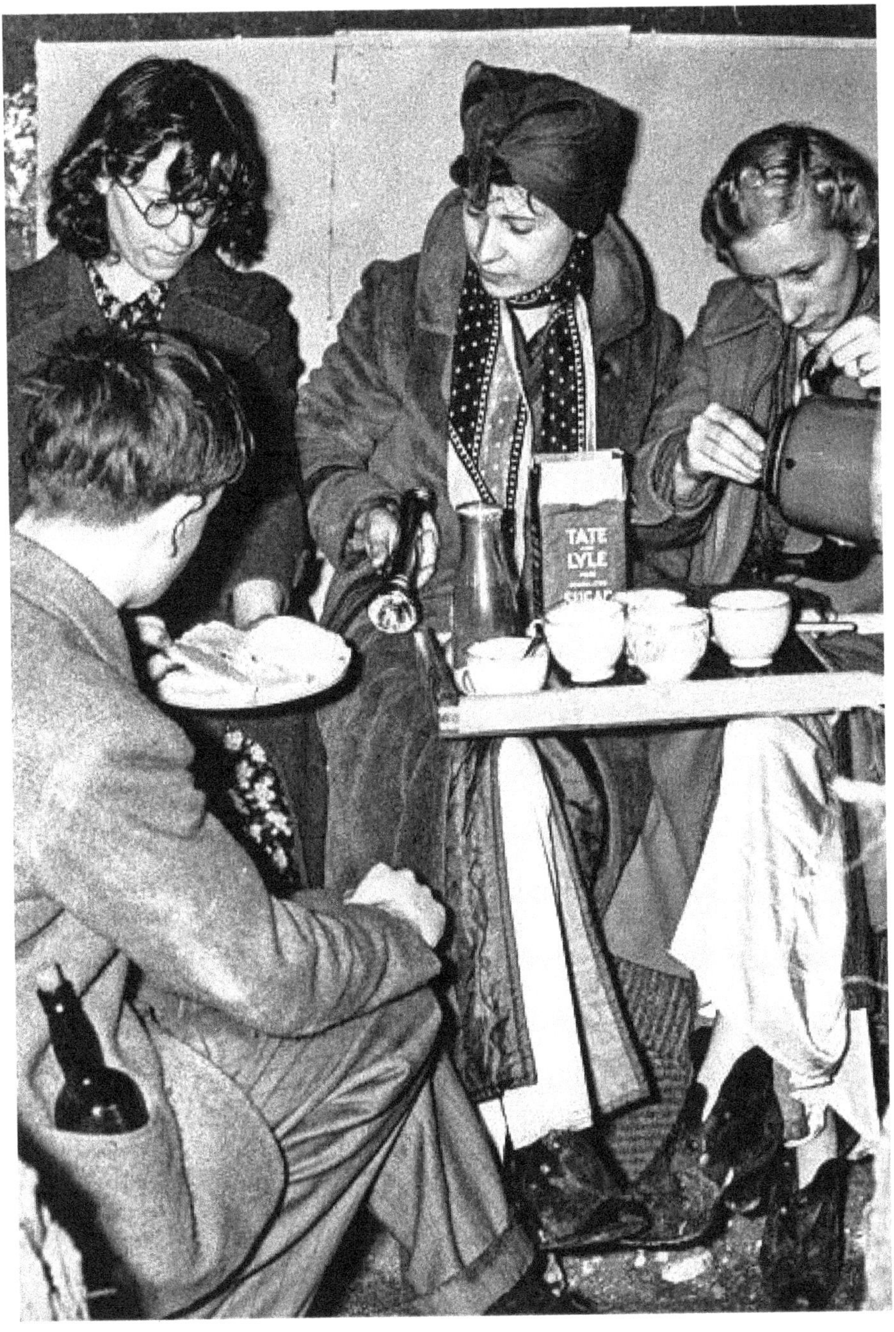
TATE
LYLE

REIDS
STOUT
WINE BAR
LUNCHEON
&
SUPPER
BUFFET
BUFFET
REIDS STOUT
MILLINERY
DEBBS
SPECIALIST
DEBBS

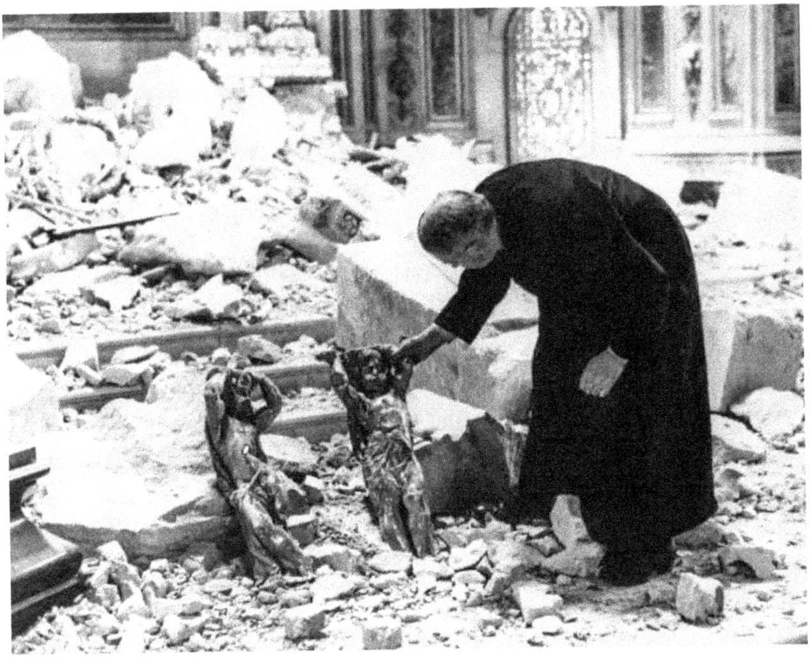

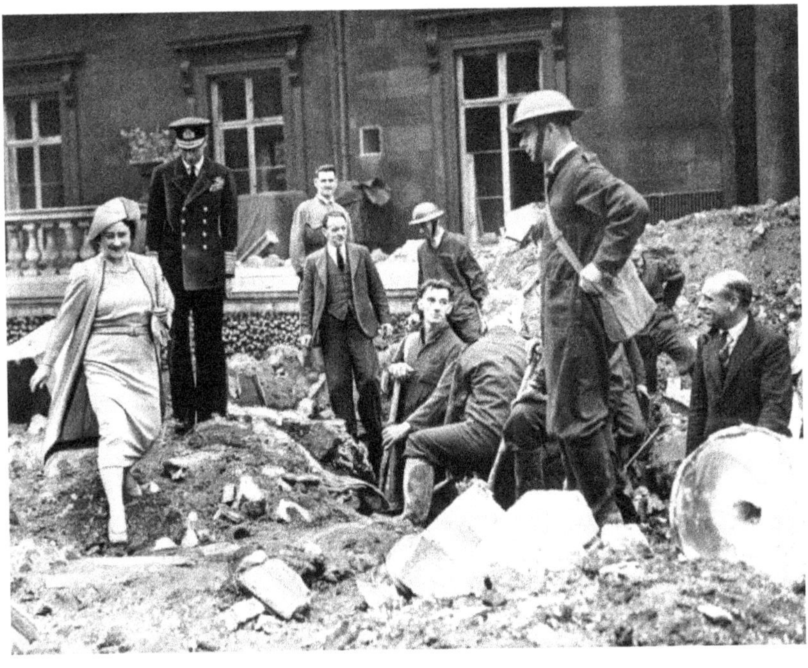

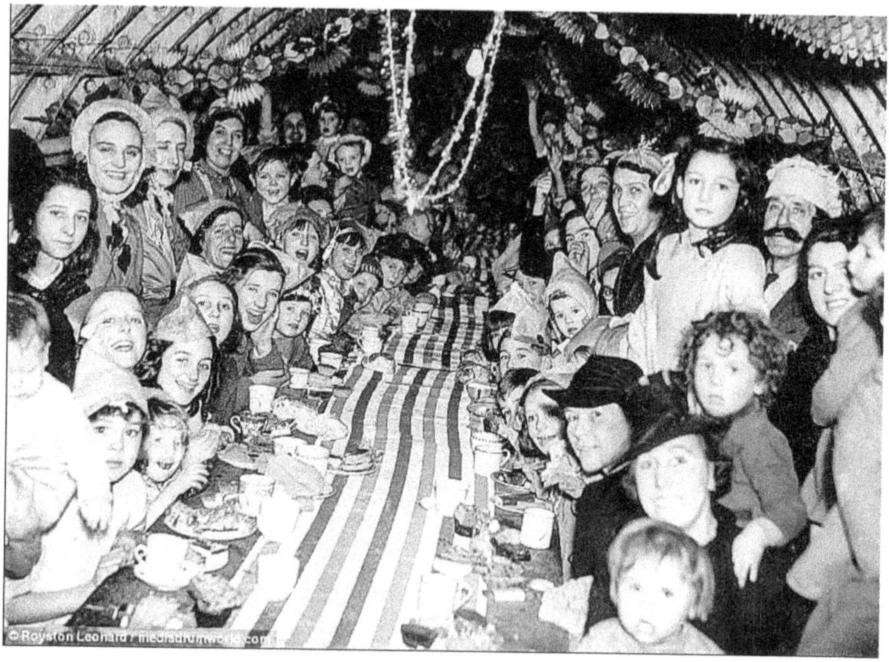

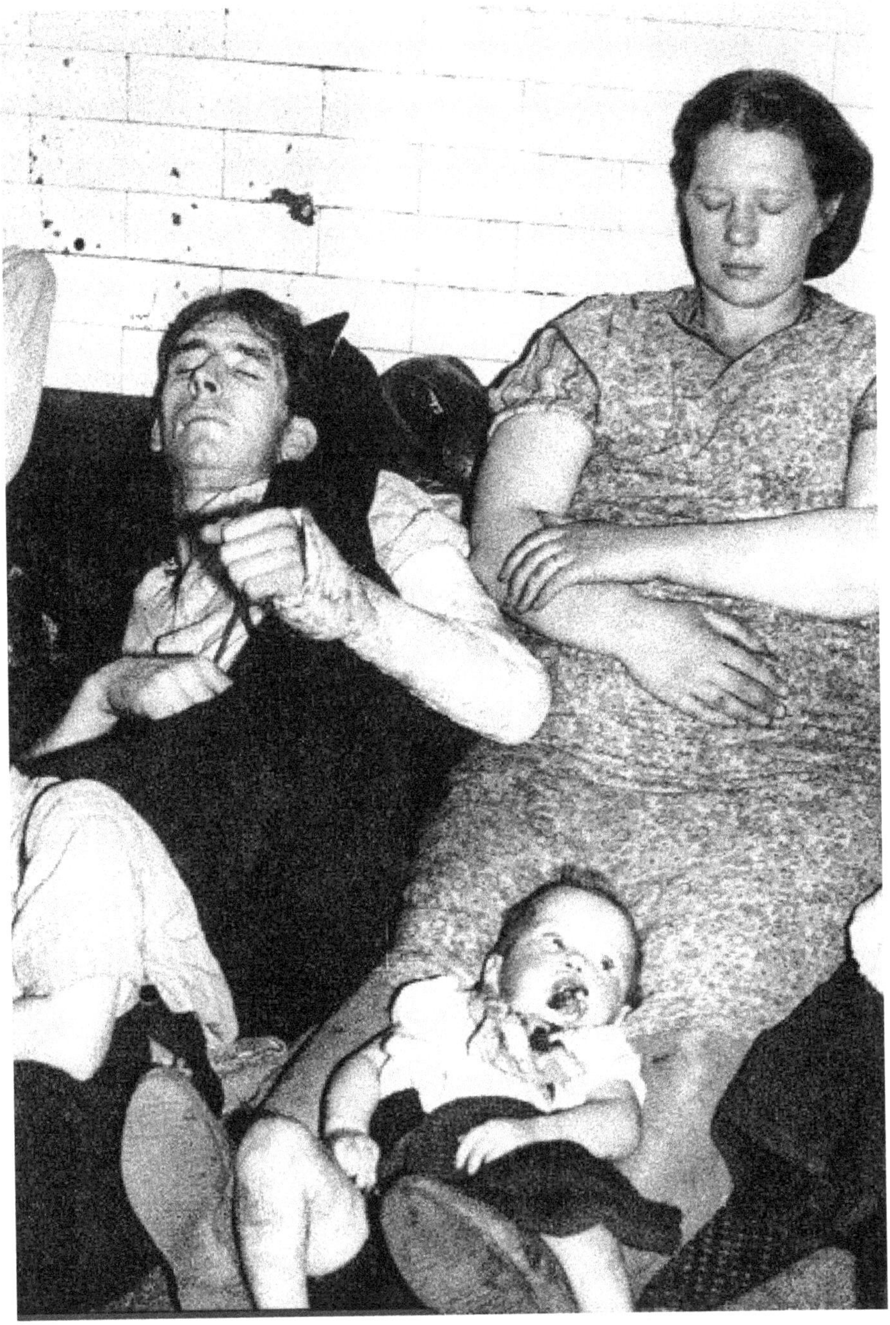

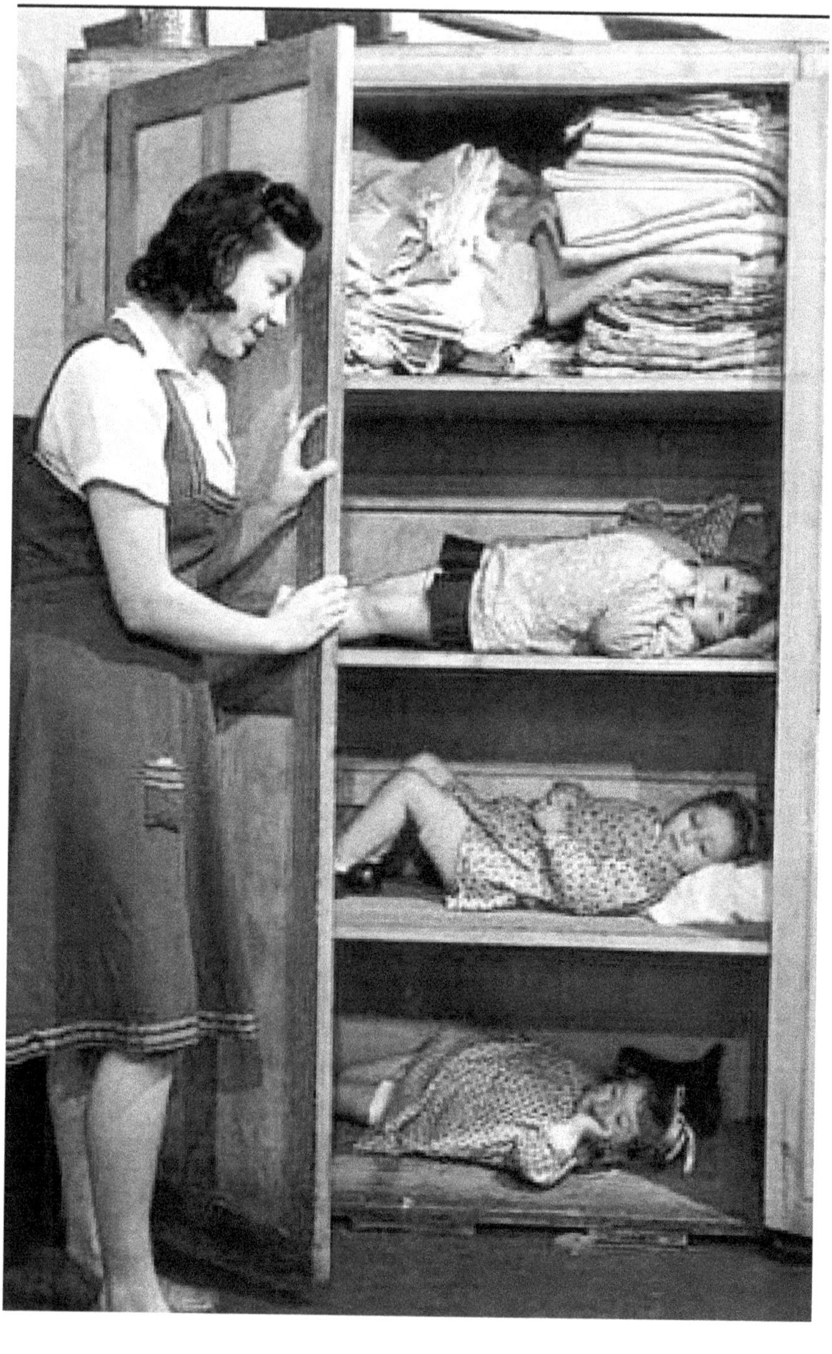

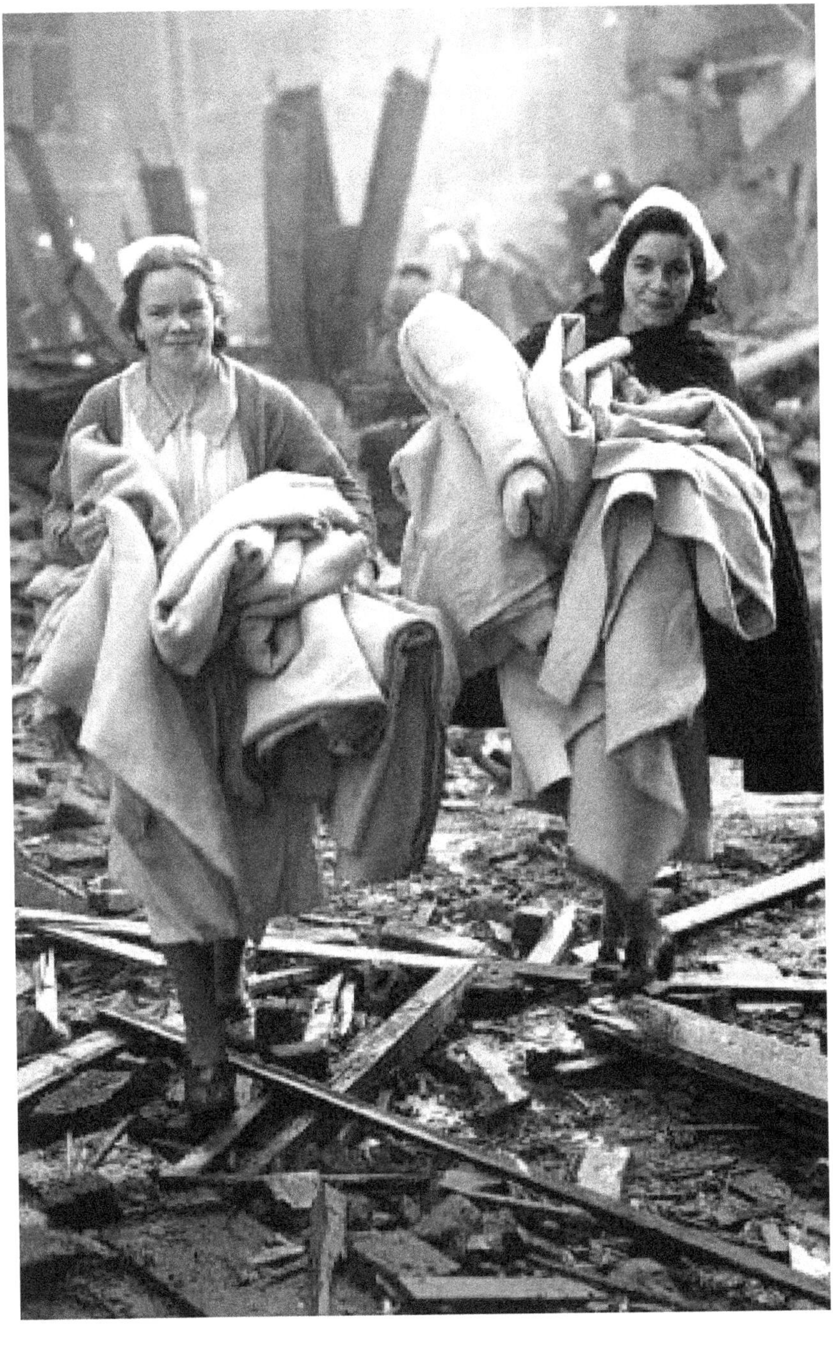

THE ILLUSTRATED LONDON NEWS

SATURDAY, SEPTEMBER 14, 1940.

ONE OF GOERING'S "MILITARY OBJECTIVES."

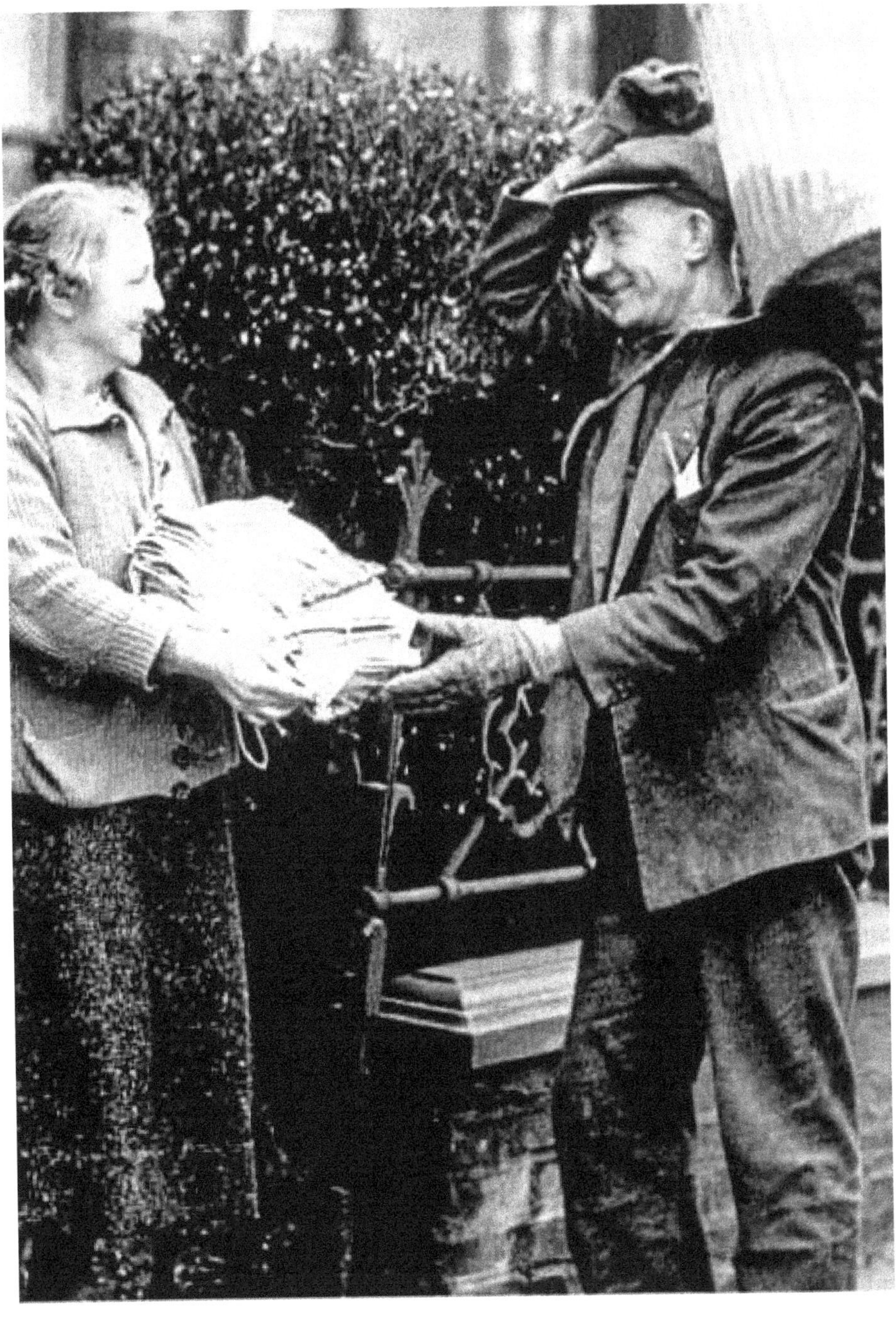

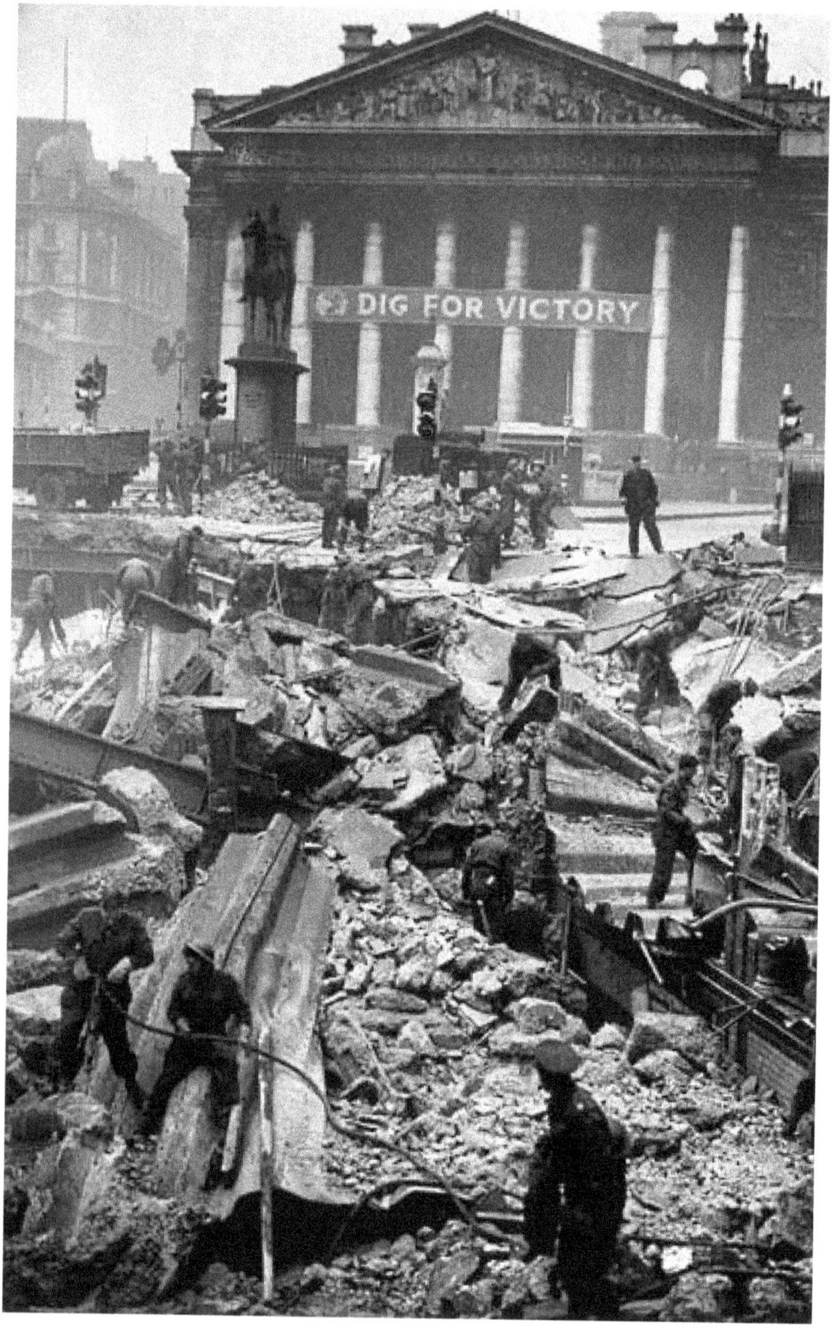
DIG FOR VICTORY

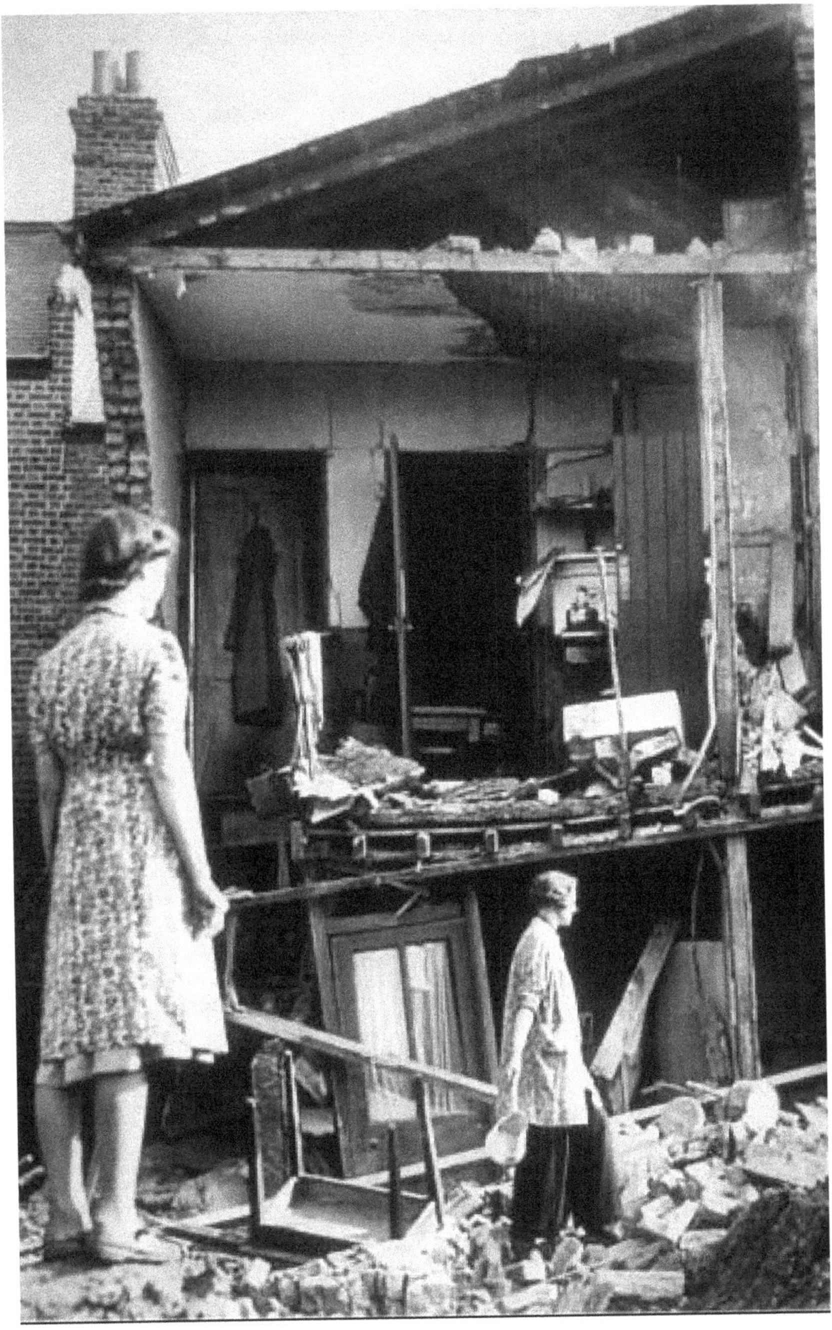

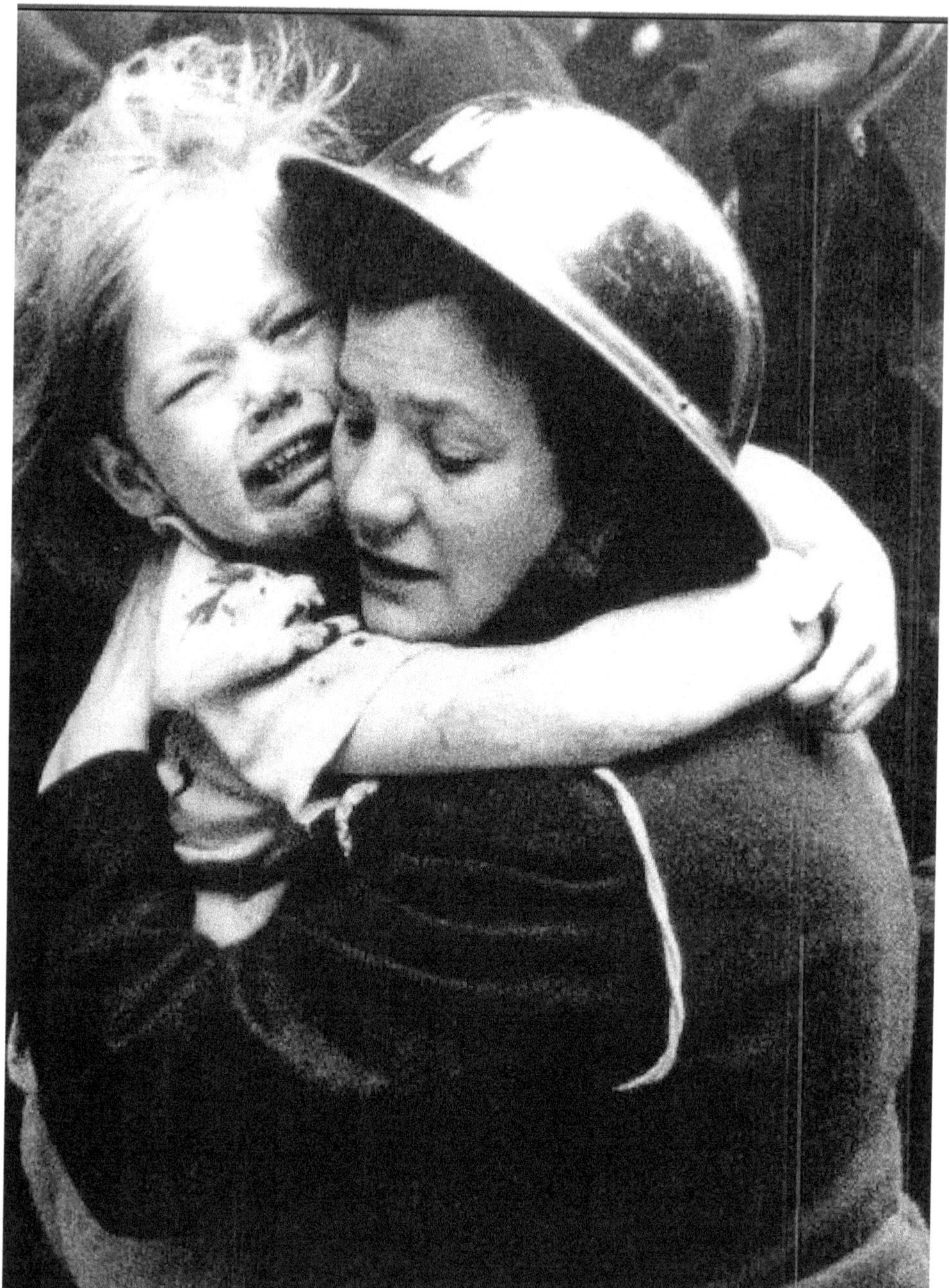

Sir John Anderson

John Anderson was the home secretary before Churchill came to power he was asked to stay on for Churchill and excepted, then he became a member of the war cabinet. Anderson was very much a philosopher and had a wealth of experience where mind meets physical body was concerned. He perhaps more than others understood the impact of propaganda which often times led to survival. He helped to establish Lloyd Georges medical scheme. *(A national insurance act of 1912 which provided compulsory insurance of lower paid workers and set a capitation fee for doctors. The government paid two ninths of the fee and the rest was made up by insurance).*

He and Churchill would often have heated disagreements with Churchill, this suggests they did not see eye to eye on a number of issues. Anderson's role as the home secretary would include law and order coupled with the fire and rescue services. The rescue effort at Hallsville School could have had more manpower so they could search relentless to recovery more victims. Anderson did not enlist earlier because of his crucial work in the government, he did go on to enlist later but was never called. When he became permanent home secretary he led the sub-committee on air raid precautions. Anderson shelters were named after him and there were more than two million made.

There was and still are numerous opinions that propaganda was the reason for the governments poor rescue effort and yet Churchill wanted a reign of terror against the Nazi's because of his nephew being captured.He used his position of power to wage a personal war and dismissed the desperate situation of the civilians in his own country.

There could have been a ban on the media perhaps preventing them reporting on civilian deaths and public damage, but within a veil of secrecy continued rescue and recovery. The turmoil Churchill was suffering, his feelings of despair and helplessness were no more relevant than the civilians searching for their mothers, fathers, sisters, brothers, children, uncles, aunts and grandparents.

To rebuild parts of the school with all those deceased under the foundations was not justified.

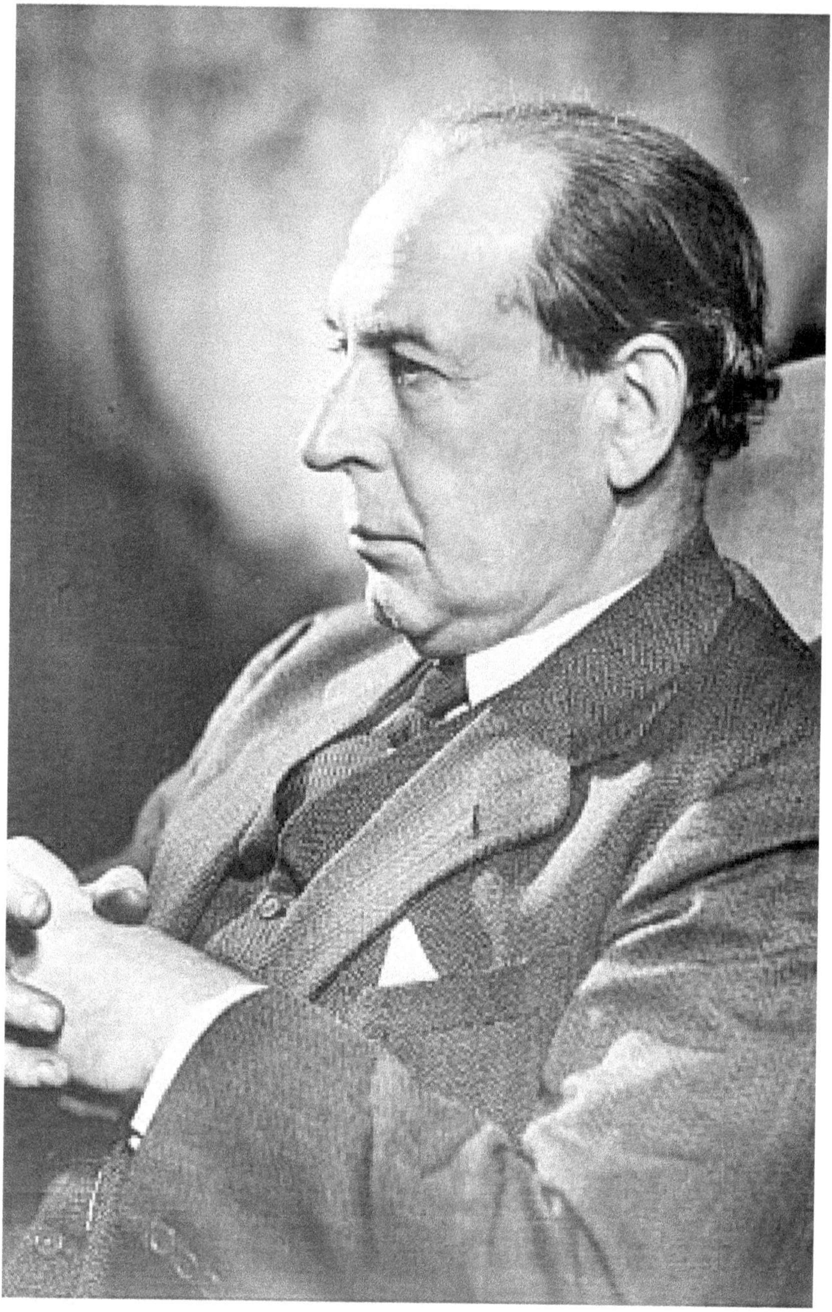

The Shadows on the Walls

There were a lot of sacrifices that civilians had to make during the war years including rationing, loss of life and of freedom. The fact that the British were called on to help provide financial support to fund the war effort and did is astonishing. This was a time when money was more difficult to earn, families were exceptionally larger so funding the war effort would have taken away from their families. Was our government that financially insecure they had to take from the working class? Many of he parliament members lived an opulent lifestyle, including Churchill. His cigars cost the government a small fortune. Cigars and stockings were only available scarcely and were prohibited.

There are still voices that can speak for the people who died. Family members and some people actually caught in the bombing are out there and have been waiting and hoping for answers incessantly. When you think about the basic concept of knowing someone you love is missing and being able to ask the police for assistance; verses someone missing knowing where they could be and not being able to get the closure is unfathomable.

That closure and a better state of mind is something we should all have and to bring out a documentary to highlight the situation but not really get to the truth enough is a second blow to the deceased and to their families.

Afterword

This story needs to be heard loudly enough to get justice in the form of recognition on a much bigger scale.

My quest with this subject will not end as this book will. I will continue to work for and with the group and their families to try and obtain a peaceful conclusion.

Lightning Source UK Ltd.
Milton Keynes UK
UKHW010628040121
376386UK00001B/218